MACHINE

LEARNING

INTERVIEWS

Stories and Tips to Crack
FAANG Machine Learning Interviews

KHANG PHAM

Contents

iv   Contents

5 Other Interview Experience and Tips   71

6 Machine Learning Topics for Interviews   97

Introduction

I'm Khang Pham, an engineer with more than ten years' experience in the software industry with two patents in Natural Language Processing.

I like Machine Learning and I love helping people. For the last two years my Machine Learning blog (mlengineer.io) and my Machine Learning System Design course on educative.io have helped thirty people get offers from FAANG companies.

In this book, I share the interview experiences from my network. I hope this book provides you with information that will be valuable for your interviews.

Good luck.

Written by An Pham
January 2022

1 Facebook

1.1 From Amazon to Facebook: Seattle 2020

Background

May 2020, E5, MLE (Offer Seattle)

Profile

YOE: 4+, all at Amazon (Applied Scientist)
Education: PhD in Machine Learning (ML) from a Top 20 CS school
Location: Seattle
Current TC: $270K
Interview dates: Last two weeks of April
Facebook offer (MLE): 205K/700K/100K

Context

Things at Amazon weren't good anymore—unclear goals, poor management, lack of communication with remote teams, etc. I decided to look elsewhere in mid-March 2020, following up with the recruiters who had reached out to me in previous years. I settled on proceeding with Microsoft, Facebook, Google, Oracle, and Indeed. Shortly afterwards, the latter two came back with the information that they were in a hiring freeze. The other three wanted to proceed, with Google even waiving the phone screen and moving directly to onsite (all the "onsite" interviews were virtual). In the following, I'll be leaving out some details in order to maintain a modicum of anonymity.

Preparation

For coding, I did the usual LeetCode grind: ~40, +20, +20 before Microsoft, Google and Facebook respectively, with about an even split of easy and medium, and a few hard thrown in. I also went through Coursera's algorithm specialization[1] (4 courses) to brush up on the fundamentals. The interviews all happened in the last two weeks of April, giving me about 4 to 6 weeks of prep time. Often, I was alternating between a day of my Amazon work, and a day of preparation.

---

[1] https://www.coursera.org/specializations/algorithms#courses

For ML fundamentals and theory, I revisited the lecture notes from all my classes during grad school, as well as the five classes in the Deep Learning specialization[2] on Coursera. I also revisited my thesis, previous published papers, summer internship projects, etc. ensuring I could talk in fair detail about anything on my resumé going back to undergrad.

For ML design, I used the booklet from the GitHub repo machine-learning-system-design[3] thinking through several of the practice design questions there. I also skimmed a few systems papers, including one I was an author on. Lastly, I used the system-design-primer to get a different view since it's not directly focused on ML.

For behavioral questions, I used resources like this list of questions from `themuse.com`[4]. For these 30 questions, and a few more I found via Google searches, I wrote down answers reflecting on personal experience and adhering to the STAR method[5].

Interviews

The phone screen involved medium LeetCode questions—a simplified version of making parentheses valid, and one about finding an index of an anagram. I received positive feedback the next day and moved on to onsite.

Onsite consisted of five interviews.

1. Coding with a Breadth First Search problem (max element on each level), and an expression evaluation problem (e.g. $2 + 3 \times 4 = ?$). I got through both fairly fast, with time for the usual follow-ups (complexity, potential optimizations, etc.).

2. ML research, and I was unsure what to expect. The interviewer was winging it a little (he switched problem statements thirty seconds into the explanation), and it ended up being more or less ML design (Instagram photo feed). I was thrown off a little since there was no documentation to structure thoughts on, and the interviewer seemed to be looking for very specific answers as opposed to a potential answer. I thought it went alright.

---

3. Coding again, with the first problem being an iterative implementation of Depth First Search, and second being the same anagram problem as my phone screen. I told him that I did this problem previously coming up with a $O(nk)$ solution, and instead of writing it out again, we just talked about how we could do better, $(O(n+k))$.

4. Half behavioral (usual affair), and half coding centered on uniformly sampling a node from a large tree. I had some difficulty understanding the objective of the problem since the interviewer didn't want me to flatten the tree or count the sizes of subtrees. Eventually I figured out the direction he wanted me to go, thanks to a couple of good exchanges between us, and I was able to write up that solution.

5. ML design, and this time, armed with a shared doc, I was able to come up with a good design for detecting offensive content in Facebook ads. I touched upon the unique aspect of adversarial design and the interviewer seemed to like that line of thought.

Outcomes

Even though the order of my interviews was Microsoft, Google (a week later), and Facebook (another two weeks later), Facebook quickly got back with what I was told was their max offer (205/700/100), and with that leverage I was able to get Google to come up to 192/900/50 by the last week of May. Microsoft offered 150/150/50 followed by radio silence.

Final Result

I accepted and signed the Google offer. Had a very amicable offer decline chat with my Facebook recruiter the same day, and I was told that the offer is on the table for a year in case I don't like my work at Google. I emailed Microsoft thanking them for their time, not expecting a response.

Summary

- Facebook asks MLE positions a lot of LeetCode questions. You can prepare for your interview as for a normal SWE position using Facebook tagged LeetCode questions.

- Review all ML concepts from multiple sources (see references).

Facebook design questions 2020/2021 and materials

Top Facebook system design questions from multiple sources: LeetCode, Blind etc.

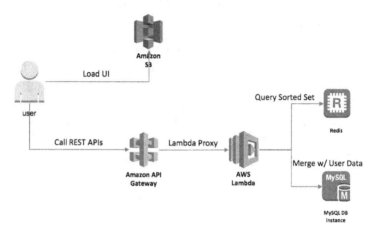

- Design hacker rank

    - Redis: Swiss Army Knife @HackerRank: Kamal Joshi[6]
    - Parallel Execution of Test Cases[7]
    - Building a Real-time Gaming Leaderboard with Amazon Elasticache for Redis[8]

- Design Live Commenting

    - Learn how Facebook builds Live commenting using ephemeral Pub/Sub[9]

- ML design feed ranking

    - How Facebook uses DL for feed ranking[10] (2021)

[6]https://www.slideshare.net/RedisLabs/redis-swiss-army-knife-hackerrank-kamal-joshi
[7]https://engineering.hackerrank.com/parallel-execution-of-test-cases/
[8]https://aws.amazon.com/blogs/database/building-a-real-time-gaming-leaderboard-with-amazon-elasticache-for-redis/
[9]https://www.youtube.com/watch?v=ODkEWsO5I30
[10]https://about.fb.com/news/2021/01/how-does-news-feed-predict-what-you-want-to-see/

- Other common use cases that you can find out on educative.io[11]:

  - Design Web Crawler

  - Design Typeahead Suggestions

  - Design Proximity Server

  - Design Instagram

  - Design Facebook News Feed

  - Design Facebook Messenger or Whatsapp

  - Design Facebook Status Search

  - Design Privacy Settings at Facebook

1.2 From Data Scientist to ML Engineer: East Coast 2020

Background

- Data scientist with 7 years of experience (East Coast, US). He talked with the recruiter mid 2020 and spent 3 months preparing for the technical phone interview.

- Position: Data scientist/ML engineer on the East Coast, US

Application

Recruiter contact in mid-2020.

Preparation

LeetCode: I solved more than 500 LeetCode questions (300 medium), most questions were Facebook tagged. One thing I found helpful was writing my solutions on the discussion section of the website, especially for questions that have poorly written solutions.

Design: I started six weeks before the interview. I spent time going through the system design topics at (educative.io), and the GitHub system design primer.

ML Design: I did three mock interviews about ML system design. During the mock intervews, we went through a variety of use cases from recommenders to ranking systems etc.

---

[11]https://www.educative.io/courses/grokking-the-system-design-interview

Behavior: I did three mock interview sessions with `interviewing.io`. I found it extremely helpful to practice with a Facebook employee. I learned how to handle difficult situations, especially when it's hard to keep pushing.

Phone Screen: All questions are from LeetCode.

Onsite

LeetCode: almost all the questions came from LeetCode. ML design questions were about recommendation.

1.3   ML Engineer Interview: Just Go with Optimal Solution

In this interview series, I summarize interview experiences from people I helped. I hope it helps you in preparing for your Facebook MLE interview. My friend got an E5 Offer. E5, NYC in 2021.

Background

- Traditional SWE interview loop with an extra ML design round. There are plenty of materials about coding and system design interviews at Facebook. All of them are accurate. The main piece of advice is to not reinvent the wheel and follow all the instructions and advice available online

- First contact with Facebook: I received a LinkedIn message from a recruiter sometime last summer. We chatted on the phone and shortly after she confirmed that I could proceed with interviews. I was pleasantly surprised by the fact that the company didn't rush me at all and was willing to give as much time to prepare as needed. I told the recruiter that I would need three weeks to get ready for a phone interview.

Coding

As you can guess, three weeks wasn't enough time to become a pro in LeetCoding. The website (as well as Reddit and other online sources) has a lot of decent posts about preparation strategies. After going through these posts and not being able to solve questions like Valid Palindrome, I decided to push back the phone round even further. During the prep phase, I developed these rules:

1. Consistency and discipline. I solved Monthly LeetCoding Challenges without taking a single day off. I was doing my prep work first thing in the morning while my brain was fresh and ready. I guess the quality of work I was doing for my then-employer took a toll but it was a trade-off I was willing to make. But if you work in a huge corporation, it won't go bust just because of one person preparing for interviews.

2. Progress tracking. I've created a huge spreadsheet to which I was adding problems after solving them. It has a following structure (below are columns' names):

	A	B	C	D	E	F
1	Name of the problem					
2	and the link	Topic	Result	Reviewed at	My code	Summary
3						
4						

Topics are tags such as "string," "DP," "backtracking," "graphs."

"Result" is whether I was able to solve it, how much time it took, etc. However, most often the value in this column was "No clue."

"Reviewed at" contains the most recent date

"My code" is a link to GitHub where I put my solution. I tried to have at least two solutions to each problem. In the comments, I would state time and space complexities and add a few sentences about how it's solved.

"Summary" is a very brief description of how to solve a question. For example, for Linked List cycle[12], I wrote: "Fast and slow: if they meet, there is a cycle."

I also added some cell coloring to highlight the most frequently asked questions for specific companies.

This set-up helped me to quickly navigate through the pile of problems I worked on.

3. Learning the basics. I strongly believe that having a CS degree isn't a prerequisite for passing a LeetCode interview. However, I did spend some time on the theory. I used the following materials:

---

[12]https://leetcode.com/problems/linked-list-cycle/

- **Books**
    - *Grokking Algorithms* (it might be too basic for most of you)
    - *Cracking the Coding Interview* (it used to be a must but not anymore, I hate this book)
    - *Elements of Programming Interviews in Python* (this one is also tough but resonated with my way of learning more than CTCI)
- **YouTube**
    - *Introduction to Algorithms* (if you want to really learn, have time and patience)
    - *Algorithms by Abdul Bari* (in case MIT is too much for you)
    - *Vivekanand Khyade —Algorithm Every Day* (a huge fan of this guy, he's so patient in his explanations)
    - *Kevin Naughton Jr* covered a lot of problems
    - *Sai Anish Malla* posts excellent explanations of LeetCode problems
    - *Back to Back SWE* might (or might not!) work for you, but give it a try

4. Talking out loud. Make an effort to learn how to talk and code at the same time, it will be helpful in any interview.

5. Specifically for Facebook, don't waste time on implementing brute-force solutions in an interview but rather move to the most optimal solution(s).

After approximately six months of studying, I scheduled a phone interview. I didn't solve the questions flawlessly[13] but did a decent job in communicating my thinking process. As such, I received an email a couple of hours later saying that I passed the round. My further coding prep wasn't much different from what I described above.

---

[13]https://leetcode.com/discuss/interview-question/974574/Facebook-or-Pho ne-or-Custom-Sort-String-and-Find-subarray-with-given-sumh

My coding questions were all Facebook-tagged. They weren't the most popular ones based on the Problems Set[14] but I came across all of them during the prep phase. I was asked a variation of "Reconstruct Itinerary"[15], "Game of Life"[16], "Missing Ranges"[17], "Word Search"[18], and others.

System Design

After I cleared my phone round, I asked for five weeks to prepare for an on-site interview. This is when I touched system design materials for the first time in my life. Overall, I found these questions easier than programming; it might be the same for anyone coming from a liberal arts background or whoever interviewed with consulting companies. A liberal arts background helps you learn to process large amounts of text, while any experience with solving cases is very applicable to requirement-gathering, driving a discussion, and presentation aspects.

- **Books**

    - *Designing Data-Intensive Applications* is a must. It's a thick book and, most likely, you won't need to read the whole thing but you definitely have to have it on your desk (or an electronic version if you have an O'Reilly subscription).

    - *System Design Interview—An Insider's Guide* has a few solved examples, and I found the author's writing style very easy to digest

- **YouTube**

    - there are many videos with problems like "Design Twitter," "Design a queue," etc. You probably want to watch a few of them and find the ones that resonate with you most.

- **Courses**

    - *Grokking the System design interview* is a must.

---

[14]https://leetcode.com/problemset/all/
[15]https://leetcode.com/problems/reconstruct-itinerary/
[16]https://leetcode.com/problems/game-of-life/
[17]https://leetcode.com/accounts/login/?next=/problems/missing-ranges/
[18]https://leetcode.com/problems/word-search/

– Classical System Design Primer[19] is a good starting point.

– This tremendous repository[20] has hundreds of links to every possible paper and article. But choose wisely, otherwise you'll never finish reading all the links.

– Another similar repository[21] with many many links.

I solved most of the common problems on my own and drew solutions in Google Drawings.

In my designs, I was followed this sequence: gather requirements (functional and non-functional), capacity estimates, basic design, discussion of bottlenecks and potential problems (mostly around scaling the solution), design of databases (if applicable), improvements to the original design, distributed aspects (sharding, caching, potential problems, such as inconsistencies if two requests from the same user land on different nodes, etc.)

I think that the key here is to be able to drive the whole discussion on your own. At the same time, I made sure I was checking in with my interviewer regularly, making sure I was on the right track. At the same time, I showed that I didn't require too much handholding and could make trade-offs and design decisions.

In my interview, I was asked to design a HackerRank-like service.

ML Design

This is probably the least covered type of an interview. Usually, questions revolve around various recommendation- or feed-based systems. Facebook has put together a Field Guide[22] that gives an accurate idea of what you need to be able to talk about. On the theory side, make sure you understand how to build scalable solutions (most likely, you'll end up with some sort of neural networks), how to handle sparse data (embeddings), and be able to talk high-level about traditional models (SVM, regressions with regularization, tree-based methods). You cannot overlook the serving portion: be ready to discuss how you will make inferences and provide a model's results to your users. Often, you cannot

---

[19] https://github.com/donnemartin/system-design-primer
[20] https://github.com/binhnguyennus/awesome-scalability
[21] https://github.com/checkcheckzz/system-design-interview
[22] https://research.fb.com/blog/2018/05/the-facebook-field-guide-to-machi
ne-learning-video-series/

run inference in real-time and need to pre-calculate your recommendations, for example. In system design, you'll come across such things as "pre-warm cache," and these approaches can be used in the ML round, too. Another topic to pay attention to is feature engineering. Be able to provide examples of features you want to build for a given problem.

- **Courses**

    - *Grokking the Machine Learning Interview* and *Machine Learning Design* from the same site are the must.
    - This repository[23] is the best starting point.
    - *Production Level Deep Learning*[24] is a great source, too. You can find a good number of links for further reading.
    - Finally, a huge list of papers and articles[25]—in case you have 6–8 months for the prep.

Pretty much every tech company has an engineering blog where they discuss various problems and solutions. Reading some of the articles was very helpful. I paid a lot of attention to the engineering blogs at Facebook, Instagram, AirBnB, Uber, DoorDash, and eBay.

In my interviews, I was asked to design various variations of recommendation engines for several newsfeeds.

Behavioral Round

To me—given my background—this was the easiest round. You can easily find dozens of example questions online and explanations of the STAR approach. Facebook interviewers were focusing a lot on conflict resolution, on examples of ambiguous projects and misunderstandings/conflicts with the peers/managers. You need to prove your maturity and ability to resolve conflicts without burning relationships with another party and without escalating. Your ability to foresee problems and stay humane are also important.

---

[23]https://github.com/khangich/machine-learning-interview
[24]https://github.com/alirezadir/Production-Level-Deep-Learning
[25]https://github.com/tirthajyoti/Papers-Literature-ML-DL-RL-AI

Practice

I've done a lot of mock interviews: around fifteen coding, between five and seven system design, five or six ML design, and between four and six behavioral interviews using my industry peers. As a result, I never had to solve a problem from scratch or come up with an example I had never practiced before.

Negotiation

I ended up with three offers. In addition to Facebook, I had an offer from another major social network, and an offer from the most popular music service. I was able to use these offers during the negotiation process and get very close to the top of the band. You can use `levels.fyi`[26] once you get to this point.

Overall, it took almost nine months between the first contact and receiving a written offer. It was great to see that Facebook was willing to invest so much time in the process.

Summary

- Practice and consistency definitely beat talent and a CS degree, at least during the interview loop. Don't reinvent the wheel, always follow the steps of those who have already been through the process.

- ML design:

    - `https://github.com/khangich/machine-learning-inter view`

    - `http://educative.io/`

    - Blogs of Instagram, Doordash, Uber, eBay

    - Videos about recommendation systems

- Behavioral questions: probably the easiest round as I'm coming from a business background and am extremely used to these types of questions. Have examples of perseverance, and your ability to build relationships without involvement of managers (or before it's too late).

---

[26]`https://www.levels.fyi/`

Keys to Success

Be able to quickly change the direction of your thought process in design rounds, if asked. Be able to talk through your code and type the code at the same time. Don't waste time on brute-force approaches, quickly move to the most optimal implementation. Do enough practice rounds so that everything looks easy and you don't need to jump above your head in real interviews. http://interviewing.io/ and my friends willing to do mock interviews were extremely important and useful.

1.4 FAANG ML Senior Manager, Offer (East Coast) 2021

Learn how to prepare for a Senior Manager interview at FAANG companies. In this interview series, I summarize the interview experiences of a friend.

Vladimir (not real name) is currently working at a FAANG company as a Senior Manager (L7+). He shared with me his takeaway from getting a very good offer for a Senior Manager position at a FAANG company.

1. How do you feel about your interview? Do you think you will get an offer?

   I don't think I got it. I think I can perform way better on the onsite. However, the recruiter came back with good news and I'm pretty surprised.

2. What to expect for Manager interview round?

   The interviewer wants to see if the candidate has handled certain situations in the past. Some situations can be really complex. I was a senior manager for many years and I have a lot of actual stories to share. My key for this round is always to come back to the relationship, i.e, how do you build trust with your reports and your team. You need to nurture the relationship over time, know your team's strengths/weaknesses and who wants to do what. As a manager of managers, you need to learn how to lead through others, and figure out what a project/product needs.

3. What to expect for system design round?

   I didn't follow the typical structure of technical requirements, non-technical requirements etc. Instead, I asked myself, given a certain use case, what are the key insights, what are one or two requirements that are critical to solve this problem and start from there. Because of that, my discussion went really deep in to the heart of the problem and the interviewer seemed to "click" with this.

4. What to expect for the Machine Learning Design round?

   Similar questions for MLE Senior level where I have to apply ML to solve one specific feature/use case. I know the building blocks and can discuss tradeoffs. It's important to be preemptive in discussing technical details, i.e, ask the interviewer if it's ok that you want to go deep in a certain area because it's the heart of the problem.

5. What are the key lessons that you learned from this experience?

   As an engineer, we're usually not very good at highlighting our achievements in the resumé. I got professional help to rewrite my resumé. It was quite expensive but it was well worth it. It's particularly important when your performance is on the fence.

Summary

- For behavior round: focus on how you build relationships with your team.

- For Machine learning design: focus on some key challenges of the problems and proactively discuss tradeoff with interviewer.

1.5   From Telecom Engineer to Facebook SWE

While taking care of two babies (source: LeetCode)

Background

Just got an offer from Facebook in mid-July; however the journey was not an easy one. Before getting the offer from Facebook, I got painful rejections from tons of other companies including Amazon, and Google. I thought sharing my story might be helpful to someone who is also struggling like I did.

My journey is little different than others. I started my career as a telecom engineer with a bachelor's degree in electrical engineering. I did not have much interest in coding at that time. I fell in love with coding gradually while building small automation tools for my team.

After 6 years in the telecommunication industry, I decided to change career and become a programmer, sacrificing my long, successful career in the telecom industry.

Start

I came to the USA and completed my master's degree in Computer Engineering. My first job as a software developer was at the University of Texas in Austin, in their technology resources department. Later, I switched to a similar position at Texas A&M University. Then in 2018, something happened that changed the course of my life. My wife completed her PhD and got her first job in Oregon. My son and my wife went to Oregon and I was badly missing them from Texas.

Deep in my heart I always wanted to be an entrepreneur and had a semi start-up at that time. I decided to leave the job, go live with my family, and use this opportunity to go after my passion i.e. try full time at developing my start-up.

At that time I had three years of experience in software development and started developing the web platform of my start-up full time. My start-up was related to higher education and ended up helping many students; however, it failed to earn enough revenue to pay my bills. I had withdrawn my 401k and invested in my start-up and at the end of 2019 I was running out of money. I had to take the tough decision to postpone my start-up and go for a job again.

All of a sudden I realized I have enough experience in running a start-up from marketing, financing, advertising to investment pitching, writing business plans etc. but that's not what most software companies are looking for.

My younger daughter was born at that time and Covid 19 broke out as well.

Preparation

I started slowly in LeetCode and started giving my full effort from January 2020. The long, gloomy winter in Oregon started with Covid 19, and me and my wife were having sleepless nights with our newborn.

During the day time, I was trying to spend as much time as possible brushing up my algorithm knowledge which I had not practiced for a long time. I was also rewriting my resumé, enhancing my LinkedIn profile, and applying for jobs.

I was not really hoping for big companies, I was not confident enough. My resumé was getting straight rejections from most of the small companies and later I realized I don't really have software industry experience and companies do not like the gap in career. I was having difficulties explaining my start-up venture which I am afraid caused most of the rejections.

However, I got contacted by an Amazon recruiter and got an invitation for an online assessment in March 2020. At that time I was pretty sure small companies would not hire me and realized big companies are better choices and hopefully they will not mind my career gap. But getting into a FAANG company is easier said than done. I spent a lot of time on the business side of my start-up and now suddenly I was thinking: can I compete with all those brightest minds of the coding world?

Easy questions on LeetCode seemed difficult to me, medium questions were impossible. I was trying hard, trying to invest all my time, after taking care of my newborn and my 8 year old son. Slowly, easy questions were getting easier and I started solving medium questions, after solving more than 100 easy questions. After solving another 100 medium questions I felt like I could pass the online assessment for Amazon, and I did. I passed the phone interview too.

Virtual Onsite

In the virtual on-site interview in April I did terrible in the system design interview (I didn't really have big scale design experience) and did medium-to-well on the coding questions. One week later, I got the rejection and did not get any helpful feedback from the recruiter about the interview. By this time I had received more rejections from a few other smaller companies. I was really getting frustrated because four months had already passed since I began!

More Preparation

I took a step back and was pondering my mistakes. I went through a lot of discussions on LeetCode and found out I am not alone. I found that many success stories have one thing in common, they stressed the quality instead of quantity, and emphasized mock interviews.

I started looking deep into each LeetCode question, going through the discussion section and trying to learn from all those elegant solutions. I started mock interviews in pr*mp. I passed the online assessment for Microsoft, but the position got postponed and the recruiter failed to manage another position for me. Five months had passed and I could not see any light of hope in the near future.

Retry

In June, I cleared the phone interview for Facebook and scheduled the onsite interview in the first week of July. I was trying to do one mock interview every day and that helped me to build confidence and improve my communication skills.

I was contacted by a Google recruiter and they skipped the phone interview and directly arranged the onsite interview. There were four coding rounds and one behavioral round. This time I did better than I did at Amazon, and at least communicated well. My mock interviews have really helped me. Out of four coding questions I solved two without hints and the other two with hints. I missed important edge cases in one of the coding rounds and I believe that bit me back.

A week later my recruiter informed me that my onsite interview was good enough to go to the hiring committee. That little feedback geared me up for next week's Facebook interview. I was at the edge of giving up everything at the end of June and Facebook was my last hope.

The Facebook onsite started with a product design interview. I was able to come with a working design and talked about different trade offs. But I ran out of time and could not talk much about scaling the design. I nailed the next coding interview. Solved two medium level questions without hints in 40 minutes and was able to go through edge cases. I tried my best in the next behavioral round. It ended with an easy coding problem which I was able to solve. In the next coding round I was able to solve another two medium level questions in 40 minutes. I made a minor mistake in one of the solutions which I fixed with the hint of the interviewer. At the end of the onsite, I was feeling really hopeful and had a feeling that if I didn't get an offer this time then FAANG probably wasn't not for me.

Three days later I got rejection from Google. The recruiter did not give any useful feedback, just said I should have done one or two rounds better. I emailed him to learn a little bit more, he didn't even reply to my email.

Now everything boiled down to Facebook. One week later my recruiter called. He told me that my coding round was really good but I could not scale up my system design. At one point of the system design interview, I asked my interviewer about his opinion instead of explaining by myself and that was a negative point. In the behavioral interview my examples were simple and they felt that I didn't have an opportunity to work in a large scale complex project which was true.

Considering all these, they offered me a rotational engineering position. Though a little disappointed, I said fair enough! My 6+ months of hard work is going to pay off finally and the desperate time is going to be over!

In conclusion, I would say, it's not an easy task to get into a FAANG company. The most important thing we need is patience and hard work. There are some brilliant people out there who can nail a FAANG interview with 15 to 30 days' preparation, but that's not true for all. Do not get disheartened reading stories of success with very short periods of preparation. Those folks are super brilliant, might have prior competitive programming experience, or excellent work experience. If you are like me, brace yourself for a long run, be patient, and keep preparing yourself! Best of luck everyone!

1.6 My Two Year Journey Interviewing for FAANG

And how to recover from burnout (source: LeetCode)

Background

I just finished my CS degree at a pretty unknown university (worldwide). One internship done in ML plus 1.5 years' experience (part-time) working as a Data Scientist for a start-up. Never did any competitive programming, also wasn't too interested in data structures or algorithms prior to February/March 2020. Location: EU. University: Also located in the EU.

My Journey Interviewing at FAANG

2018

This is when I really "discovered" FAANG and what it meant to work there. I started applying to every single internship I could find. The only one to reach out was Facebook.

The phone interview was a total disaster. I had a very bad internet connection and had done almost no preparation (I hadn't heard about LeetCode back then). Obviously, I received no offer then.

2020

February

I applied to some new grad/junior roles. The only ones who reached out at this point were Google. I scheduled an interview for March so I'd have time to practice, and then had to reschedule for April due to personal issues.

On the 25th of February I signed up for LeetCode. For about a month, I did 1 or 2 problems on average per day (some days I did none, some days I did 20). At this point, I had barely any memory of any data structure that isn't a string, tree, dictionary or array. I mean, I did remember the general ideas about lots of DS's, but I had zero practice. To better understand my situation, I avoided all graph and tree problems for the first month, as they were too complicated for me.

March

I did two Online Assessments for Amazon, they finally reached out to start the interview process for a Solution Architect position. A few days later I got an automated email saying they wanted to proceed to a phone interview.

Phone Interview

Wasn't sure what it was going to be about. I ended up having to answer a lot of network related questions, a bit of basic algorithm trivia and a lot of behavioural questions. I wasn't asked to write a single line of code. Answered all but two questions (more than 20) quickly and clearly. Behavioural-wise, I had read a lot about their principles and was prepared to answer all the questions that he did ask. I thought I did really well, the interviewer seemed very pleased. Was sure I was going to get to the onsite round.

Result

One week goes by, no news. I checked the career website and the position was archived (No longer under consideration). Another week later, I got an email saying they won't proceed with my application.

My Feelings

Overall I was disappointed with the whole process at Amazon. E-mails were all automated, and there was little recruiter contact. Also, the fact that nobody reached out to tell me they won't be moving forward with the application (had to find out a whole week prior to the automated email that was sent to me) made me pretty happy they said no. To be honest, I was given the feeling that candidates don't mean anything to them—and are treated as just an expendable resource. Won't be applying there again in the future.

The failure at Amazon made me miserable for a few days, but then it gave me a lot of motivation to do better in the future. This is when I started LeetCoding pretty seriously (19th of March is when the grind started for me).

April

The Google interview was coming up, I was LeetCoding for at least 5 hours every day, and reading chapters from Corman's *Introduction to Algorithms*. Some days everything made sense, and I would do even 20 problems or more a day. But other days, especially when faced with a new topic, I could barely solve one or two problems.

So I decided to get a yearly premium subscription for LeetCode, thinking that if I do get the job now, I won't care about the money and it will have been well spent. If I don't get the job, I'll need the subscription in the future. It was a win-win for me. I mainly wanted this to see which kind of problems will be given and to take advantage of the solutions provided and of the mock interview feature (specific for companies).

Google

About a week before my interview, besides LeetCode, I started doing mock interviews with my friends and I can't stress this enough: THEY REALLY HELP. It was great being able to do this first with familiar faces, and I was able to see how I'm reacting under pressure and learned how to gain control of my emotions.

A few days before the interview I read a LeetCode article from someone saying they'd contacted their recruiter one year later and they ended up getting an interview, so I decided to email my recruiter from Facebook from the year prior, hoping to get an interview. She redirected my email to another recruiter, who was happy to schedule an interview for me.

Phone Interview

Had solved about 150 LeetCode problems by then. This interviewer was so nice, we joked a lot, talked a lot. Really nice guy. The problem statement was something on the lines of: Given two dictionaries, merge them into one.

I asked a lot of questions and came up with a lot of solutions, most of them of the same complexity. Ended up talking a lot about each of them and wasting too much time with that. Realized 20 minutes in, that I hadn't a single line of code. Panicked, decided to just start implementing one. Coded it right on the first try. After testing, received a follow up about nested dictionaries. Spent a lot of time discussing what I'd change, didn't realize how much time I'd spent. Changed my code very quickly, barely managed to go through one example before time ran out. Also didn't have time to write an auxiliary function that I said I'd use, but I explained it very carefully.

Towards the end of the interview, I felt like I was just doing a mock interview with one of my friends. It was very genuine. The interviewer even said he had a great time during the interview. I had a pretty good feeling about this interview too.

Result

One week later, recruiter calls me to offer feedback. Said I was really close to making it, and that they love my personality and I definitely have the "google-iness". Told me that I should manage my time better, and that they decided to say no this time because I spent too much time explaining stuff. Also said the interviewer was impressed with how fast

I wrote the code, but he thought I needed "a few more months of real-life experience" to make it at Google. Had a really nice chat with him, and he urged me to stay in contact and reapply for that specific job in a year, but said he'd be glad to hear from me for other job openings in the future (I mentioned I wanted to apply for a new grad position in the fall).

My Feelings

Was pretty bummed, not going to lie—not even making it to the onsite rounds. Especially since my best friend made it (she had very similar DS&Alg knowledge with mine, in some areas better, in some worse). And by this time, both my boyfriend, my best friend, and another close friend had gotten jobs at Amazon and Microsoft. I was feeling really behind (and kinda dumb).

May—Burnout and No Time

Final exam session, had very little time to LeetCode. My Facebook interview was scheduled for the middle of June, knowing that I would have very little time to prepare in May. Did maybe 1 or 2 problems every other day. Sometimes I'd do more on weekends.

I applied to some other companies, had a few interviews in May, June & July, none FAANG, none special or worth mentioning. It was great to have more interviewing experience, I'd advise everyone to apply for as many positions as they can, it's great practice.

June

Since I had little time to prepare the month prior, I set my goals to only make it to the onsite round—and I'd be happy with that. I was already thinking about reapplying in the fall once all the new grad positions would re-open.

I had very low motivation to do anything following these previous failures. But I did anyway. Not as much as before, I was feeling the burnout more and more.

Facebook Phone Interview

Had solved about 220 LeetCode problems by then. Won't be giving too many details, but there were two problems, one data structure design, and a very common LeetCode question that I'm sure all of you already know.

Got an email two hours later informing me we'll be moving on to the virtual onsite round. We scheduled for 1.5 weeks later. I had reached my goal. I was so happy.

Unfortunately, I had some issues which resulted in me spending half the time left before my interview in bed, sleeping. I did do some problems the days before the interview, but at this point the burnout was too much to handle and I was at peace knowing that I'll do my best, and if that's not enough right now, it's okay.

Virtual Onsite

Won't be giving any problem specific details since I signed an NDA. Had solved about 240 LeetCode problems by then.

- Round 1: Behavioural only. I got one problem to solve. As soon as I saw the problem I knew exactly how to solve it (hadn't seen it before, but it was nothing too difficult). Interviewer seemed pleased, but couldn't really read him.

- Round 2: Coding. This one was by far my favourite interview ever. The guy was the nicest ever, we had a lovely time chatting and I think our personalities really clicked. I also realized how to solve the problems pretty fast, also wrote the code pretty fast. Had time to go through examples, optimize and all that. In hindsight, I think this interviewer was my biggest advocate, it really felt like he was my friend.

- Round 3: Coding. I was so happy with how the first two rounds had gone, and I went into the third interview with a lot of confidence. And I met an interviewer with whom I simply couldn't click: I'm very talkative, he wasn't. I generally need feedback or reassurance before I take any decisions or change stuff (I ask things like should I start implementing this, or do I try to find something better). The first problem I did right. Forgot about an edge case, realized during testing, changed my code. At this point, I really started thinking I might get the job.

- But behold, the last problem. It wasn't hard by any means, but I had no idea how to solve it optimally. I spent around 15 minutes trying to come up with good solutions, none worked. Interviewer informed me I had 5 minutes left. I said "I give up, I'm sorry, I can't solve this better, I'll do the bad solution I previously mentioned". Wrote it in literally 2 minutes, only had time to write some tests, not actually go through them and verify my code. Ultimately, the code worked. But I felt I reached a horrible solution (complexity-wise) and that I spent too much time on trying to find something better—and failed at it.

My Feelings

Was so bummed after the last interview. Everyone kept telling me about how high the bar is at Facebook, and how they want you to do everything perfect. I was sure they were going to say no. My best friend had an interview for the same position two months prior. She had the impression she did everything right, was expecting an offer, and then they said no. So how could they say yes to me, since I had "failed" so bad at the last problem (meaning it wasn't perfect).

Spent the next two weeks convincing myself I wasn't going to get it. I was 99% sure there was no way they'd say yes. I refreshed my email almost every 15 minutes, waiting for them to send the email, putting me out of my misery.

July—Result

Recruiter sends me an email saying they're still gathering the feedback, but that she'd call me on the phone the following week.

She calls, starts by thanking me for my interest in Facebook and for my effort. This is exactly how rejections are formulated most of the time, so it was going exactly how I thought it would. Thirty seconds into the call she adds "all these being said, you did great in your interviews and we'd like to offer you the job". I was speechless. Honestly, I feel so blessed.

All I want to say is that I know job searching is a struggle, and that burnout is a real issue. And sometimes, rejections feel like the end of the world. But they're not. And I'm the living proof that it's possible. You just need to do your best. I'm not by any means a competitive programmer or someone who has been doing this for a long time. Four months ago I had no idea how to use a heap.

But hard work (paired with just a little bit of luck) always pays off.

TL;DR

Rejected by Facebook 1.5 years ago (because I was a noob). Rejected by Amazon & Google. Big burnout. Three months of grinding and 1 or 2 of doing LeetCode now and then. Interview at Facebook, thought I wouldn't pass the bar, but I did.

Advice

I really hope this motivates some of you guys! Just keep working and what's set aside for you (like, in the big scheme of the universe) will eventually be yours. Just do your best and don't give up!

Contacting Recruiters

I set up one of those alerts on the Google career site for when a new job based on your criteria shows up. The timing of when you apply is very important. If you apply for a job that's been posted a month ago, chances are they're already interviewing a bunch of candidates. But if you apply for a job that's been posted yesterday, it's much more likely that someone's gonna read your CV and give you a shot! (same applies for most companies).

If I had to do it again, I'd just go on LinkedIn and search Google/Facebook/Amazon Recruiter, and send out connection invites to as many people as LinkedIn will let me. Then, for those who respond, I'd write them a message saying who I am, what my background is and what kind of roles I'm interested in, and then ask for their help. I know people who did this and it worked for them.

Once you get the email of a recruiter, you can pretty much keep emailing them from time to time asking to be considered for a job, or to be referred to somebody who'd consider you for a job.

My advice would be to create a network as big as possible on LinkedIn and to make sure that you have all your information there and that your profile is attractive to recruiters, then reach out to them yourself. Pretty sure at least 10% would respond, and you only need one recruiter from a company to say yes, and then getting interviews in the future should be much easier.

Recovering from Burnout

I tried taking a mental break from all of the things that were stressing me out. Had about a five day period in which I did absolutely nothing. Then I tried to get back into it slowly. Couldn't keep up with the expectations I set for myself, so I set new ones. Also, I tried to do things that made me happy, and to give myself time. It's important to be patient with yourself, I can't stress this enough! I also tried meditating and that helped a lot. Sleep enough, drink a lot water, go outside. Best advice I ever got! And remember why you're doing what you're doing, what the end goal is. Or try to find something that motivates you.

Failure

A lot of people at big companies failed! Failure only tells you how well you did at a specific point in time, it doesn't define you, your knowledge or your capabilities. Some people spend years applying for the same role, and then they make wonderful software engineers.

1.7   I Practiced 2 LeetCode Questions Per Day

There are many ways to get an Facebook MLE offer. I found this one on the LeetCode discussion area, and I think this is very attainable. I hope it helps.

All questions I was asked were small modifications of questions I found in the "Facebook" section of LeetCode's Explore. I highly recommend using LeetCode Premium for that reason.

Background

- Experience: 3.5 YoE in developing computer vision and NLP models + PhD from a good school.

  Position: Deep Learning Engineer at a FANGMULA company (not telling which for anonymity, sorry).

- Current TC: $260K

  Facebook Offer: $205K/620K/100K (base/RSU over 4 yrs/sign-on)

- I contacted a recruiter on LinkedIn, after looking for a recruiter specializing in ML.

Preparation

- LeetCode: I did one or LeetCode questions per day for half a year (workdays only lol). My final count was about 60/70/20. At first, I did the 50 easy questions with highest frequency. Then I went through all the LeetCode $\longrightarrow$ Explore $\longrightarrow$ Facebook questions. In the month before the interview, I did very few new questions to avoid losing confidence. Instead, I focused on redoing medium and hard questions, this time explaining what I'm doing aloud.

- Design: Started two weeks before the interview (but had a fair amount of real experience at work). Read a system designer primer[27] and all the material the recruiter suggested. Then, I designed one large system per day on a whiteboard, speaking aloud, during the week before the interview.

Phone Screen

Two questions, both LeetCode medium level. One similar to Anagrams[28], one an easier version of Remove Parentheses[29].

Onsite

- LeetCode round: a highly modified version of Number of Islands[30]. One Specialist Ninja round: [edit: this is also a coding round! but not LeetCode coding :) for example, it could be "implement precision/recall calculation" for general ML or "normalize images" for computer vision folks] Can't say the exact question; I do not want to dox myself. This round is supposed to catch people who don't do on a daily basis what their CVs suggest they do. So don't worry unless your CV is fake.

- System Design: One focused on NLP and one on a general ML system (similar to "design Facebook newsfeed"). The NLP Specialist design round was really "tell me roughly how an NLP model fits within the larger system, and then focus on all the different models/tradeoffs, how to eval/monitor them etc". 70% talking about the model.

---

[27]https://github.com/donnemartin/system-design-primer
[28]https://leetcode.com/problems/find-all-anagrams-in-a-string/
[29]https://leetcode.com/problems/remove-invalid-parentheses/
[30]https://leetcode.com/problems/number-of-islands/

- HM round: Tell me about a time you had a difficult coworker—
  what did you do? Tell me about a time you shaped your team's
  direction. etc. This round is what will decide whether you're E4 or
  E5. IMHO, it's very hard to fake it. My preparation was thinking
  very carefully about all the "politics" I encountered in my current
  job. In daily work, instead of avoiding difficult situations, jump
  right into them and try to help. It's very easy to gather great
  E5-type experiences in this way, even with as few YoE, as I have.

Negotiation

I knew Facebook bands from Blind. I just told the recruiter to ask
for max band, and said I'll cancel other interviews if they get close
enough (>200/600/100). She returned with 205/620/100 and I accepted.
Didn't have any competing offers, but was in the final stages of another
FANGMULA loop.

Additional Comments

In the phone screen, I came up with a suboptimal solution (NK
instead of $N \log K$) to one of the problems. It didn't matter because I
communicated well and wrote great code. During the onsite, I totally
messed up the LeetCode round and started solving the wrong problem
at first. Halfway through, after many hints, I figured I'm doing the
wrong thing. I made sure the interviewer knew that I realized I'm wrong,
and why I got confused. Then went on to solve the right problem by
modifying the original solution. All the time I was very careful to keep
the interviewer involved. I'm not sure if she had another question to ask
me or not; I only solved one because of this mess up. Guess what? It also
didn't matter. The recruiter said all interviewers were very impressed.
Communication is very, very important. You can do 1000 LeetCode
questions but will fail if you don't communicate well. Interviewers know
everyone grinds LeetCode, they're looking for soft skills on top of that.
I've interviewed almost 100 candidates at FANGMULA, trust me on this.
The same goes for system design. You can't just memorize a bunch
of charts. The best way to train these is to seek out opportunities to
communicate with your peers during real-life work. Talk about your
ideas and code, write docs, draw diagrams. In meetings, don't be the
person sitting quietly in the corner.

Also, try to do a lot of interviewing yourself. It really helps.

1.8   Most Common Coding Mistakes According to Facebook Engineer

Learn from a Facebook interviewer who has conducted hundreds of technical interviews.

Source: aleksandrhovhannisyan.com

What are the most common mistake that candidates make during coding interviews?

Candidates mostly validate their logic and don't validate their code, hence they are not able to find bugs in their code. Candidates don't follow a systemic approach while coding. They jump between places and add checks in a haphazard manner.

How to avoid this mistake?

Be sure to validate your code by following it line by line. Adopt a systematic approach, think through and then start implementing. The benefit is to avoid syntactic mistakes, handle edge cases, and verify output. You can see an example in this video. It only takes 5 minutes to watch and can save you months of preparation.

Please practice validating your code line by line with some input before grinding your LeetCode.

What are the two signals that Facebook interviewers are looking for in coding rounds?

Able to adapt design to follow up questions. Show understanding of data structures that they use.

Is it ok if candidates know the problem/solution and just write their answer right away and finish their questions in 10 minutes? Is it a bad thing since the interviewer will realize that the candidate already knows this question?

It is okay to do so, but be prepared for follow up questions. For example, if you use a complex data structure such as a heap, the interviewer can ask you to implement a heap.

Summary

- You should practice validating your code line by line.

- Practice how to adapt your design to follow up questions.

- This is my LeetCode tracking sheet. Most questions are from Facebook. I tried to practice each question three times.

2 Amazon

2.1 How I Got Data Scientist Offer During the Pandemic

Ted Vic is a Senior data scientist working in one of the coldest place in the US (MN). He's the first person who score 9/10 on my ML quiz[1]. I hope it helps you in preparing for Amazon Data scientist interview.

Application

I applied using a referral from a friend for three roles that I was interested in. A recruiter reached out to me within a week for one of the roles

Interview Rounds

- Two Phone Screen Interviews and Five rounds of virtual onsite loop

- Phone Screen—The first round consisted of a live SQL coding round on coder pad, and theoretical questions to test machine learning and statistics breadth knowledge (Eg. lasso vs ridge, bias-variance tradeoff, etc). In this round I was to build a simple ML pipeline from data wrangling to model building using R/Python. The second round included behavioral questions based on Amazon's 14 Leadership Principles (LP) and a walk through of a past project that the interviewer was interested in.

- Virtual Onsite Interview—six hours duration. The interview consisted of five rounds of 60 minutes each with a one hour break

- Round 1—This round tested the breadth of machine learning and statistics knowledge with several quick definition/quiz type questions just like the phone screen round 1. It was 30 minutes. The other half of the round was behavioral with focus on few LPs

- Round 2—This round focused on the depth of Machine Learning with a case study. I was given a problem statement and had to walk through my approach starting from data cleaning to deployment

---

[1] https://mlengineer.io/machine-learning-assessment-db935aa9fafd

of the model in a scalable way. The last few minutes of the round was, again, behavioral with focus on few LPs

- Round 3—This was a coding round focused at data munging and writing code to answer questions using data. I was given a choice between R/Python/SQL. The second half was behavioral just like all other rounds

- Round 4—This was completely a bar-raiser round which was entirely focused on LPs

- Round 5—The final round was focused on testing my ability to write scalable Python code for data munging which tested Regex, etc. Just like all other rounds there was some time dedicated to LP

Preparation
- SQL—I completed all the hard SQL questions from LeetCode. Another resource that I used for refreshing Window functions was `https://www.windowfunctions.com/`.

- Python—I was tested on my ability to build an end-to-end ML pipeline using Python including a lot of data cleaning. I did not prepare much for this because of my experience in previous roles. If you are not confident, I would recommend that you work on this by practicing on a few datasets and reading through some popular kernels on Kaggle. Be ready to provide solutions which can scale to large datasets with hundreds of features and millions of rows

- Behavioral—As you can guess from my experience above, behavioral questions on Amazon's 14 leadership principles (LPs) carry a lot of importance. I would recommend that you prepare multiple events that touch on the LPs that are important for your role; these can be guessed from the job description. Be prepared to answer follow up questions that dive deeper into the story narrated by you. Also, you can be asked a similar question by multiple interviewers and you are expected to narrate a different experience as much as you can. I went through some of the videos in a playlist by Dan Croitor[2] and it helped me a lot for my preparation. Thank you, Khang for sharing this resource with me :).

---
[2] `https://youtube.com/playlist?list=PLLucmoeZjtMTarjnBcV5qOuAI4lE5ZinV`

- Machine Learning and Statistics—There are a number of resources for this on the internet. The way I prepared for this was by reading about all the techniques/algorithms that I had used/mentioned on my resumé. I also ensured that I covered all the basics of statistics and machine learning which included linear regression, t-test, bias-variance tradeoff, evaluation metrics (pros and cons), loss functions, etc. StatQuest by Josh Starmer[3] helped me a lot to refresh my knowledge. There are some ready to watch playlists like Statistics Fundamentals, Machine Learning, etc that cover most of the basics in a very simple way

- Past Projects—For this I ensured that I worked on stories about most of my projects on my resumé. I prepared for some questions listed below, at least for the work that I had done in my last organization or were relevant to the role that I was applying for:

    - What was the business problem that I was trying to solve
    - The data that was available along with any interesting feature engineering
    - Different approaches that I had thought about or attempted
    - Some of the challenges that I had faced
    - How did I deploy the model?
    - Details about the experimental setup, if an experiment was conducted to test the model
    - Any ideas that I had for further improvement

Key to Success

Apart from the preparation above, I would recommend encouraging an attitude similar to that of a memoryless system on the day of onsite interview. The interview is very tiring so it is very important to maintain your composure throughout the process. I felt that I did not do well in my first round but I managed to keep my cool till the end which helped me crack this interview

---

[3]https://www.youtube.com/user/joshstarmer

Negotiation

Unfortunately, the team I interviewed for decided to go for another candidate for the role. However, as I had cleared the interview bar, the recruiter helped me find a team that I was interested in. This process took around two months and I was given an offer after an informational interview with the new Hiring Manager. I used `levels.fyi` to get an idea about the salary ranges for my level.

2.2   How I Got Data Scientist Offer Within 2 Months (2021)

Learn how to prepare for the Amazon Data Scientist interview

In this interview series, I summarize interview experiences from people I've helped with interview preparation. Patrick is a Senior Data Scientist working in one of the coldest place in the North America. I hope it helps you in preparing for the Amazon Data Scientist interview.

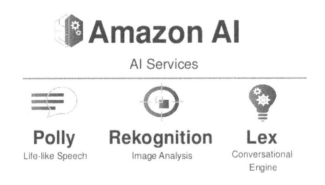

Source: Amazon AI

Application

The process was for DS L5 (received at the end) and was started by a referral. The entire process took about four weeks.

Preparation

Screen with the recruiter (0.5 hrs). We chatted about my background, what I'm looking for in the next role, and why am I applying now. Do not underestimate initial phone screens in general. I have gone into some calls unprepared thinking that my resumé speaks for itself, having this "I'm in demand" mentality, only to be rejected outright. Before a call, I always make sure to follow the following structure to answer the 'about me' question:

- Introduction: 2 or 3 sentences. First sentence states my credentials, the second sentence describes what drives me and what I'm passionate about as a data scientist, third sentence highlights my top skill(s) as a data scientist.

- Body: Include two high level examples of past projects that prove your selling points in part (a). Be very concise, don't get too technical, but include keywords from the job description as needed.

- Conclusion: Rephrase your key points from part (a) and end it off with one or two points indicating why you are specifically excited about this opportunity with this company.

In my experience, the recruiter will almost always ask you some form of the 'about me' or 'tell me about yourself' question at the outset—don't worry about the specific wording of what they ask, just pretend you heard the words 'sell me yourself in three minutes' and hit them with a well prepared elevator pitch. If you are well rehearsed, then this step will boost your confidence for the remainder of the call and hopefully they already decided to put you through the process at the introduction. Prior to the call, I make sure to fine-tune my selling points to include keywords from the job description where applicable and basically "throw back" the exact qualifications at them, this way there is no room for interpretation and they hear the keywords coming from me directly. Note: do not recite the JD, but wrap up the key words from the JD in a unique story about yourself and your experiences. This takes a bit of practice but once you get used to it a few times it becomes routine.

Other notes: make sure you also prepare answers for questions like "why us?", "why now?" and "what are you looking for in your next role?" Lastly, prepare one or two questions for the recruiter to show your interest.

Technical Pre-screen (1–2 hrs)

In depth discussion about past projects. In my experience they gave me the option to choose what to dive into. Their intention is to figure out how many levels deep you were involved with this project. Be prepared to answer questions starting from "what was the business objective?" all the way to "why did you decide to derive example weights like X and not Y in your loss function?" They will ask you things like why you chose the models that you chose, what candidate models did you consider, what were the trade-offs? They can go quite deep here so make sure you are familiar with the example you decide to discuss. If you hit a level that was out of your scope (this is pretty much a certainty), then admit it and don't BS them—no points lost.

At the end they ask a coding question but not LeetCode style. It tends to be some practical data manipulation question using either SQL or Pandas.

Onsite (5 × 1hr)

This is the onsite round which you either have for a straight 6 hours (5 + 1 hr break in between). Here are the rounds in no particular order:

Bar Raiser

This is usually with a senior member at Amazon and they will ask you several LP questions and then ask follow-up questions based on your answers. The preparation for this is quite laborious and exhausting but beneficial overall if you apply them to interviews with other companies as well. My preparation was as follows

- I mainly consulted `https://interviewgenie.com/`. This website lists all LPs, describes what they mean and what interviewers are probably looking for, then lists a bunch of possible questions related to them.

- I compiled a Word document with a table of contents of about 30 questions and answers. This takes a while, because you're forced to really reflect on the learnings in your career. Make sure you write your answers in STAR format. During the interview, I will highlight the questions that I already used so that I don't double dip accidentally.

- During the interview, every time I was asked a LP question, I asked for 30 seconds to look through my notes for an example; once I found one, I would have it written in STAR format and refer to it. This gave me confidence while answering and I didn't waste valuable preparation time and brain space memorizing answers. Interviewers know and expect that you will have notes written down and reading from them will not result in points deducted.

- What I've learned

The LPs are not mutually exclusive, for example one of your "Invent and Simplify" answers might be very applicable to a "Dive Deep" question and that's completely fine. While it is advised not to use the same answer more than once during your loop, I found it was ok to use the same situation for different questions but focus on different aspects of that situation. For example, I had one situation that involved both a "invent and simplify" component but also a "disagree and commit" component so I recycled the situation but gave different answers to two separate interviewers.

While there may exist dozens of questions for an LP, the essence of each one is captured by one or two core components. Therefore, don't get caught up writing answers to 100 LP questions, prepare maybe two or three for each one and just be sure to address the components of that LP. For example, "Disagree and Commit" boils down to having a divergence of opinion with a team member but then also committing to one of your opinions—therefore I prepared two stories: 1) a time when I disagreed with a team member and we went with my idea 2) a time when I disagreed with a team member and we went with their idea. "Insist on the Highest Standards" is looking to see how you wouldn't accept a "good enough" or "status quo" way of doing something; what were your motivations for going above and beyond to change it and how did it benefit the business or customer.

Make sure you include stories of when you failed. This is very important because having only success stories makes you look disingenuous and does not give the interviewer an idea of how you deal with adverse situations.

Science Breadth

This section tests you on a lot of different concepts but not on a deep level. Questions can be simple definitions, or some high level concepts related to work you've done. Some questions can also be presented in the form of a simple case exercise such as how would you process a dataset for training and how would you decide what model to use. Interviewers at all rounds will always ask follow-up questions to your answers so if you suggest an idea or approach, be sure you are familiar with it. They may also ask you about keywords you wrote on your resumé. For example, if you wrote "GANs" somewhere on your resumé, don't be surprised if they ask you to explain GANs to them in detail with a bunch of follow-up questions. Make sure you brush up on fundamentals of ML and statistics—reading through some comprehensive material can help with this, Analytics Vidhya[4] has a good one.

Science Depth

This section is more specific to your background. You will likely be asked to dive deep into a technical project you've worked on or a concept you're very familiar with. In my experience I was asked about the first bullet point of my most recent role, so make sure you are very familiar with your resumé because they will go deep on one thing for about 45 minutes. In many ways this was similar to the technical pre-screen described above.

Science Case Study

This is usually with a HM and they will ask you an open-ended question on how to solve a real world problem related to Amazon. Since I signed an NDA I will not share the details of this interview—however—in preparation for this I reviewed several sections of the course *Grokking the Machine Learning Interview* on educative.io. I followed this structure when approaching the problem and the discussion went very well:

1. Repeat and clarify the initial problem statement to the interviewer.

---

[4]https://www.analyticsvidhya.com/blog/2018/06/comprehensive-data-science-machine-learning-interview-guide/

2. Define the metrics (if applicable, define both online and offline metrics) that you will use to measure the success of your proposed solution.

3. Describe what features you will consider for building your model(s) and how you will engineer them.

4. Describe how you will generate your dataset: how you will select an unbiased sample, deal with class imbalance, consider temporal effects. How will you split into train/val/test?

5. After you train your model, discuss how you will backtest before deployment.

6. Last step is discussing how you will monitor real-time performance.

This is a flexible guideline because the interviewer may ask questions in between to guide you in the direction that they want you to go, so it's entirely possible that you won't hit some of these points and that's totally fine. Just read your interviewer and be open minded to go down whatever path they're hinting towards—make sure to always have a structure in mind and you should at least cover steps (i) and (ii) at the very beginning.

Data Manipulation. This was some basic data manipulation questions —you may use SQL or some other language of your choice. I made sure to brush up on my Pandas skills and SQL skills (mainly stuck to SQL on LeetCode).

Other Insights

How much do you prepare for LeetCode? How many questions did you solve? How many weeks/hours did you spend on LeetCode practice?

As a data scientist I practice more LeetCode than necessary for personal reasons. I have completed 178 problems (90/83/5) and completed most sections of the *Grokking the Coding Interview: Patterns for Coding Questions* on educative.io. I spend at least 3–4 hours/day, 4–5 days/week LeetCoding during the job search. In my experience, all companies I interviewed with asked easy/medium (60/40) LeetCode for data science. Only one company ever asked me more advanced data structures and algorithms—they were looking for a full stack senior data scientist.

How do you prepare for SQL?

I don't spend much time practicing SQL because I am comfortable with it from my day job. Before an interview if I know that there will be a SQL component then I practice a few medium/hard SQL on LeetCode.

If you start again, what is the one thing you want to do differently in terms of preparation?

In hindsight, I actually tripped on a few basic stats questions during the Science Breadth round (I literally just forgot the definitions of some basic concepts), so I would've brushed up a bit more on stats fundamentals.

Do you find mock interviews helpful? In terms of ML knowledge, which books/resources you find helpful?

I have not participated in any mock interviews, but I will in the future. One helpful resource for the Science Breadth round is a comprehensive guide on Analytics Vidhya[5]. I would read through these as a refresher of concepts and if I wanted to dive deeper on something I'd just YouTube/Google it, or refer to old course notes from school. I also consulted Andrew Ng's courses.

In total, how much time do you spend preparing? At which point did you realize that you're ready for the onsite?

I don't spend X hours preparing, during a job hunt I just practice at every opportunity that I get until bedtime, weekdays and weekends. I don't ever feel fully prepared for an interview, because they can ask you anything—I think the key is to be persistent and keep learning. I will stop learning new concepts two days before onsite and accept that "I am confident in the things that I know at this point" so that I don't overwhelm or stress myself out with unknowns too close to the onsite. Until the onsite, I just review what I already know and maybe look at some new concepts if I feel comfortable. I noticed that every time I go through a job hunt, the first onsite is the most stressful. Next time I will do mock interviews before the first onsite to break the ice.

---

[5]https://www.analyticsvidhya.com/blog/2018/06/comprehensive-data-science
-machine-learning-interview-guide/

One last thing to consider is to trust your preparation. If you were persistent and diligent in your preparation, then trust that your brain will be able to tackle some tough unexpected questions during an interview.

2.3   Amazon Applied/Data Scientist Interview Question 2019-2020

I personally collected a list of questions for Amazon Applied Scientist and Data scientist positions. This list excludes LeetCode questions, domain specific questions, i.e, Automatic Speech Recognition, NLP and Computer Vision.

1. How would you compare the results of two different search algorithms? How would you incorporate the rankings of the results?

2. Explain bagging versus boosting and write code for different types of search. Which binary search algorithm is the most efficient?

3. Write Python code to return the count of words in a string Coding test: moving average Input 10, 20, 30, 10, ... Output: 10, 15, 20, 17.5,...

4. SQL: Write SQL to return the cumulative sum of top 10 most profitable products of the last 6 months for customers in Seattle.

5. Assumptions about logistic and linear regression.

6. Explain collinearity. How to treat collinearity?

7. Given a bar plot and imagine you are pouring water from the top, how would you determine how much water can be kept in the bar chart.

8. What are the assumptions for using logistic regression? What is the loss function for it? How would you build a recommendation system in certain scenarios?

9. Designing recommendation system for Amazon website, model choices, evaluation criteria, and reasons why these would be the best choice.

10. How do you find the parameters in logistic regression.

11. What is the difference between L1/L2 regularization.

12. Pros and cons of random forest and why.

13. Given a generator of unbiased Bernoulli numbers (0 or 1 with $p = 0.5$), create a biased Bernoulli trial generator (generate 0 or 1 with the specified $0 < p < 1$).

14. Differences between bagging and boosting.

15. How does GMM/HMM work?

16. How does PCA work, and what's the physical intuition.

17. How does K-means work, what kind of distance metric would you choose, what if different features have different dynamic range?

18. If you have large number of predictors how to you handle them?

19. Modeling question: what if you have large number of positive observations vs few number of negative observations?

20. How to write a function to make a biased coin from a fair coin and vice versa.

21. Forecast: Difference between Holt-Winters method and ARIMA.

22. Explain SVM, how to choose a model, and how to determine if one model is better than another.

2.4   How I Failed Amazon MLE Interview

I only did 60 LeetCode questions.

I feel this post might help people who are interviewing at Amazon. I have taken some of my time to post my experience.

Online Assessment: (March 17)

- Articulation points

- No of islands

- LP questions (MCQ)[6]

Phone Screen: (March 31)

- Two LP questions with a LeetCode medium coding question on graphs. Interviewer seemed professional.

Round 1

- Interviewer joined late

- 20+ minutes of behavior questions

- OOAD + Coding: Got only 15 minutes to do this coding question. I was able to give the solution in $O(N)$, he expected better. Never saw this question on LeetCode

Round 2

- 30+ minutes of behavior questions

- Coding: LeetCode hard question, I was able to give him the solution and this round went well. Interviewer seemed professional

- Q&A for 5 or 10 minutes

Lunch

Round 3: Manager

- Interviewer joined 5 minutes late

- 30+ minutes of behavior questions

- Manager was in a rush and we didn't have time and started system design. I used http://draw.io/

---

[6]https://leetcode.com/discuss/interview-question/344650/Amazon-Online-Assessment-Questions

- System design easy question but the manager was actually questioning on every single statement I uttered. I was explaining trade-offs and reasons for each of my statements but at one point he asked me three questions; it was tough for me in that pressure moment to memorize his questions and explain everything in detail.

I kind of got screwed in this round. I think my post my might help people to get prepared to handle those situations.

Round 4
- 30+ minutes of behavior questions

- LeetCode medium question (in 20 minutes)

- Q&A 5 to 10 minutes

Round 5: Bar Raiser
Sixty minutes of LP. I did very well in this round. As she was a senior manager in data science, she asked a few questions on my project and on data engineering stuff as well. Interviewer seemed very professional.

Result
Rejected

Overall Experience:
- I felt from the discussion with the bar raiser and in the phone interview that the interviewers seemed very professional and positive.

- Got rejected at OCI onsite. I was interviewed for senior applied scientist this February. I got rejected because of not meeting behavior values of OCI. This time I prepared LP's hard and got rejected because I am from DS background and should have practiced system design better.

- Position at Facebook is on hold. I had been disappointed for last few days because of the rejections I had been receiving over the last few months

My Details
4 YOE as MLE, tier 2 company.

My Preparation

- LeetCode premium 20 easy, 25 medium and 15 hard (I just practised the patterns)

- DS and Algo ND (Udacity)

- System design scalability I used `educative.io`'s Scalability & System Design for Developers learning path[7]

- Pluralsight (Design Patterns course).

- Object Oriented Analysis and Design (Head first Book)

- Literally I spent almost 40 hours from March 17 in preparing LP's because I thought if not L5 I will get L4 if my LP's are right. But the manager mentioned he only wanted L5, not L4 at this moment (Indirectly). I regret that I should have invested that time in actually doing system design instead of reading the book.

Last Thoughts:
I think you guys can easily clear the coding rounds with the practise you have on LeetCode. Thanks LeetCode for getting me this far. Last September, I found it tough even to work on arrays and linked lists. Looking at this amazing community, I got motivated and was able to reach this far. My worry is that currently no company is as actively hiring. Should wait for the future and hope the best happens.

2.5 How I Prepared for Amazon Applied Scientist (L5, 2020)

My friend is a PhD with 4+ years of experience at non-FAANG company. He recently joined Amazon as an Applied Scientist. He shared how he prepared for the onsite interviews.

---

[7]https://www.educative.io/path/scalability-system-design

Amazon Interview

How much do you prepare for LeetCode? How many questions did you solve? How many weeks/hours did you spend on LeetCode practice?

I did close to four months of rigorous practice on LeetCode. Solved 300+ new questions and also revised 350 previously solved questions.

Do you have a system design round? Do you have SQL questions? How do you prepare for it?

No system design. Only ML design (phone and also onsite)

If you start over again, what is the one thing that you will do differently?

Practice more LeetCode and also prepare more on ML design

I personally collected a list of questions for Amazon Applied Scientist and Data scientist positions. This list excludes `mlengineer.io`

Do you find mock interviews helpful? In terms of ML knowledge, which books/resources you find helpful?

I think mock interviews help and I underestimated their importance. Books: `http://d2l.ai/` (deep learning AI online book is awesome resource); kdnuggets articles are also very useful; Chip Huyen's blog is also very resourceful, `https://huyenchip.com/blog/`

In total, how much time do you spend preparing? At which point did you realize that you're ready for the onsite?

Four months of rigorous preparation was needed. I would probably aim for six to be very confident.

Below is his experience with Facebook and Google reposted from LeetCode[8].

Facebook Interview

Facebook Recruiter reached out and I had phone screen in December: Standard two medium LeetCode questions from Facebook tagged top 100

---

[8]`https://leetcode.com/discuss/interview-experience/1094860/facebook-e5-m l-bay-area-reject-google-mtv-swe-ml-14-15-waiting/879366`

with minor variations and I was informed next day that it went well and I scheduled my onsite in late February.

Virtual Onsite

- Coding 1: Two Medium LeetCode questions from Facebook tagged top 100 with minor variations. Interviewer seemed happy at the end as I was able to code both of them and run through test cases. Seemed interested in an extension of second question to large data which cannot fit in memory. Asked to write basic functions for this extension but we were out of time so I spoke of an idea.

- Coding 2: Two easy LeetCode questions from Facebook tagged top 100 with minor variations. I did the first one well adjusting for the variation but I did a slight mess up in the next one which I believe cost me the interview.

- Behavioral: Standard questions and one LeetCode easy—I believe this one went fine.

- System Design: Was asked a design question not from G course or general Facebook System Design questions. I went through my design and the interviewer was mostly patient to let me lead it by interrupting as and when further clarification was needed. I did put an architectural drawing in Google drawings (spoke of components in the design for availability, partitioning, consistent hashing, priority queues, etc) while talking completely throughout the interview.

- ML Design: I was asked an open ended question to design a recommendation feature for Facebook. I tried to explain all the details to interviewer who seemed to nod his head all along. He finally mentioned that the design makes sense. He also said he was taking notes so I can continue explaining without writing/drawing the design. I had a decent connect with interviewer and I thought this round also went well. I believe I made a mistake here also by letting the interviewer take notes based on my explanation rather than me write them in Google drawings myself. (It's tough to say which option is better as each has its pros and cons)

Interview Experience

Overall, the interview was well conducted and interviewers were polite. In general, I felt I did well except for the minor mess up in coding round 2, second question. I have seen folks mention that behavioral and ML design are key for E5 in ML which did go well for me, so I was positive.

Recruiter sent a one line rejection email within three days with no feedback whatsoever.

This is very disappointing to see a company like Facebook behave like this and expect the candidate to re-apply within one year when you are not giving any feedback for rejection in the first place. I have had rejections before also where a recruiter would at least call and speak for five minutes to go through the feedback. I have reached out to the recruiter for feedback but I am not sure he will respond. I have seen similar behavior by recruiter for another Facebook E5 post here, but did not expect this would happen to me.

Here is some feedback for folks interviewing for E5 ML:

- Coding: Even a small bug means in one question out of 2 or 3 questions implies you have lost that complete round. You need to finish two medium LeetCode's (with extensions if possible) and run through test cases completely by the end of the interview to stand a chance.

- I did not find the ML folks to be technical enough at Facebook, so folks with significant knowledge in ML should definitely answer the design questions in an extremely dummified way.

Google (L4-L5 ML SWE)

Advanced directly to onsite, possibly due to good performance in previous onsite 3 years back.

- Coding 1: Two LeetCode medium problems but not asked as usual LeetCode problems. Google interviewers might present it as an ambiguous question. I was able to do well here and the interviewer was really nice. He gave confirmation of the same.

- Coding 2: Very open ended coding question which was ambiguous and needed communication to understand which data structures to use. Again nice interviewer and I think I did a decent job in here.

- Behavioral: Standard behavioral grind. Tried to answer naturally as I had prepared

- ML 1 : Very unusual ML question which needed to write code for a Bayesian classifier (again this was hidden in the ambiguity of the question). I resolved the ambiguity and came all the way to a Bayesian approach but could not write the code for the classifier due to lack of time.

- ML 2: Lots of discussion on CNNs and how to apply them to a real-world problem.

- ML Design: Design a feature for Google search. I did put all my thoughts in the Google document while talking through but the interviewer seemed a bit puzzled by my approach.

2.6 I Prepared Amazon and Facebook ML Interviews for 6 Months

In this interview series, I shared my friend's interview experience.

Background

Steven (not real name) got a Master of CS with 6 YOE in consulting. He applied to multiple companies but only got replies from Facebook and Amazon. He went onsite for both companies.

Facebook Research Scientist Onsite

- Data Science Coding round (45 minutes)—Build a model for classification. Focus ML modeling from end-to-end.

- ML Design—It was quite complex problem that needed to handle text and image data.

- ML Theory, Probability and Statistics: some applied stats questions, i.e: Bayes theorem, Central Limit Theorem, confidence intervals. They also asked about other data science and machine learning questions.

- Cross functional round

- Behavioral

- LeetCode

Sample Questions
Kth Largest Element in an Array[9] and Merge sorted arrays[10].

Amazon Senior Computer Vision Scientist Onsite
Most questions are about: GAN Model how to train and how to evaluate, attention-based model, auto-encoder and when do you use it. Explain my GAN projects. Explain other advance network architecture, i.e: Residual Nets and LSTM.

Deep Learning questions: How do you handle issues with deep learning models? How do you do regularization in deep learning? Difference between L1 and L2 regularization and when you use each of those? Some concepts about computer vision in 3D.

Feedback and Result
Recruiter said I have strong knowledge in computer vision, machine learning and deep learning overall, but lack some deeper experience in these areas. They needed more experience from past. Recruiter said I'm not suitable for this senior computer vision scientist position.

I don't recall leaving any direct question on computer vision or deep learning left unanswered or incorrect, but there was so much leadership principles-based questioning which I did talk about ML projects. It was not good enough.

Nothing lined up now.

How Did I Prepare?
I did some Facebook tagged questions mainly from the top of the list both sorted by most frequently occurring and also in their default order. I also followed courses on `educative.io` about grokking coding patterns and grokking dynamic programming coding patterns.

---

[9]`https://leetcode.com/problems/kth-largest-element-in-an-array/`
[10]`https://leetcode.com/problems/merge-sorted-array/`

A day before I would just revise patterns and do one question of every type.

2.7 Amazon Applied Scientist Interview (Europe, 2021)

Background
   Master of CS with 3 YOE.
   Onsite interview, there are 5 rounds.
   Tech talk : presented one research project I did

Coding :
   • https://leetcode.com/problems/house-robber/

   • https://leetcode.com/problems/fruit-into-baskets/

ML Depth
   Questions about NLP, RNN, LSTM, BERT (how does it work? Self attention? How is it computed?) etc...

ML Breadth
   More general questions, classical algorithms, maximum likelihood estimation, maximum a posteriori, overfitting etc ...

Problem Solving
   How to build a search engine? Which methods to use? Choice of features etc. Check whether reaching the end of an array is possible given each position has a number of steps you can go forward. Serialize–Deserialize a binary tree

ML Questions
   Bias-variance tradeoff. Unsupervised learning (k-means application and handling unlabelled data). Spam filtering approach.
   There were general discussions about using models in text, information retrieval in practice as well.

How much do you prepare for LeetCode? How many questions did you solve? How many weeks/hours did you spend on LeetCode practice?

Two weeks of preparation : ~50/60 easy and 25/30 mediums using this website : https://seanprashad.com/leetcode-patterns/

How do you prepare for ML breath? How deep were the interviewers' questions about Bert, deep learning?

For ML breadth mainly ISL + ESL are sufficient. For BERT I had questions about the architecture, what is bert? and they asked to explain the self attention mechanism, how is BERT trained, why transformers are better than LSTM? etc.

If you start again, what is the one thing you want to do differently in terms of preparation?

I think the key is to start way in advance. On the ML breadth and previous projects, I was good. So I think that I need to :

- focus more on problem solving, LeetCode, complexity calculation (it can be tricky with some problems that involve recursion) etc.

- have a better knowledge of some classic problems in the field that I'm applying for, (for example in NLP, knowing about search engines, recommendation systems etc.)

In total, how much time do you spend preparing? At which point did you realize that you're ready for the onsite?

Two weeks (5 to 7 hours a day) because I didn't know about LeetCode before. I never felt ready because I only had two weeks to prepare.

3 Google

3.1 I Only Solved 200 LeetCode Questions for L4 Position(2021)

SC has background in Computer Science with 4 years of experience. He got a Google Software Engineer, Machine Learning position (L4) in East Coast. He wants to share his experience for others.

Do you focus on companies tagged specifically?

Only the week before an interview for that company. The frequency tags were fairly accurate for Amazon, Facebook, and Two Sigma but Google used fairly unique problems I haven't seen on LeetCode before.

How many questions did you solve? How many weeks/hours you spent on LeetCode practice?

All said and done, about 200 questions on LeetCode. I feel I over prepared. I focused my efforts on mostly medium problems and occasionally would "blitz" five easy questions in 30 minutes. Spent some time on hard questions, but not much. I did probably 10 hours a week for two to three months. Probably did around 50 LeetCode questions during actual interviews since I spoke with a lot of companies.

If you start again what is the one thing you want to do differently in terms of preparation?

I think I did a good job of preparing and I wouldn't change anything.

What other tips would you recommend?

Learn all of the fundamental data structures and algorithms so that you understand them fully. Do NOT learn DS&A specifically in terms of solving LeetCode problems.

Solve problems based on different patterns. Then when you get a problem in an interview, identify what pattern it is. For example, understand Two Pointer patterns and recognize palindrome problems as frequently using Two Pointers.

Keep notes of small tips that can come up for improving time complexity. Obvious example—caching with hashmaps/dictionaries. Less obvious—anagrams can be solved $N \log N$ with sorting. Or you can do in

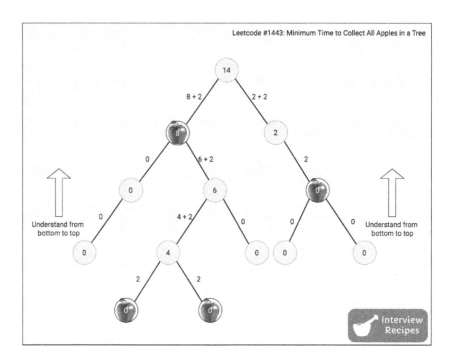

Leetcode #1443: Minimum Time to Collect All Apples in a Tree

$O(N)$ by caching with a counter using multiplying of primes or storing with an array of counts.

Do you find mock interviews helpful? In terms of ML knowledge, which books/resources you find helpful?

Doing mock interviews if you have never interviewed before would definitely be beneficial, but I have done so many LeetCode style interviews now that I feel like I have it down pat and wouldn't invest in it now.

3.2   I Spent 3 Months for my Interview (L5)

Adam is a Senior SWE with 5 YOE after his PhD in ML. He took my course ML System Design on educative.io[1] and used it for the Google ML system design round. He was kind enough to share his tips with us about how to get a Google offer for Senior SWE, ML position.

---

[1]https://rebrand.ly/mlsd_launch

What kind of ML design questions did you have? Is this recommendation, computer vision or something else? Do you need to know unsupervised learning?

I was asked ML system design problems that are similar to those on `educative.io`. I didn't prepare unsupervised learning, but depending on the interviewer, you can be asked any question, so having breadth in your knowledge will help. I think the primary focus is on being able to walk through your solution systematically and not get lost in the complexities.

You should be able to explain in detail about how you would build the components of your ML system and then evaluate it when it is put in production. The ML System Design course on `educative`[2]/GitHub[3] is a must have resource in this regard and allows you to visualize how things fit in.

How difficult is the system design? Is it similar to Grokking System Design or something else more niche?

As I had applied for SWE ML roles, I only had ML system design rounds

How do you prepare for ML rounds since there are many topics to cover?

I spent a month studying ML—for me setting a deadline and schedule of topics/papers for each day provides motivation to power through despite the large amount of material to study. I tried to finish my preparation a few days before the onsite to allow my mind to relax a bit. Although I have prior background in ML from grad school coursework, I was a bit rusty on the details.

I spent a week or so reading through relevant chapters of the textbooks by Bishop (PRML), Hastie et al. (ESL), and Goodfellow et al. (DL) to get the fundamentals right. Coursera also has good videos on topics such as DL and ML which I used for brushing up on concepts. Stanford's Information Retrieval and Mining of Massive Datasets course materials are also very good for recommendation systems/search engine fundamentals.

After this, for the remaining 3 weeks, I read papers and company blogs related to different ML problems—for instance object detection/seg-

---

[2]`https://rebrand.ly/mlsd_launch`
[3]`https://github.com/khangich/machine-learning-interview`

mentation/recommendation systems etc. These resources do a good job explaining the rationale behind choosing a specific method of modeling the problem. I tried to avoid Medium blogs when possible since there is a lot of noise/inaccuracy there.

To test my concepts further, I tried to solve the same problems on my own, and this helped me identify topics I did not understand fully. After enough papers, you start seeing similarities and understand the trade-offs between different approaches, and this helps you pick the right tools for attacking any problem during the onsite.

Finally, I did some mock interviews with friends a few days before my onsite to practice following a systematic approach to ML design in a time constrained environment. I got a lot of useful feedback in these mocks that helped me refine my approach.

How many months/weeks do you spend preparing for the Google round?

Overall, around three months. I spent 1.5 months ramping up on LeetCode till I hit ~250 problems, and then switched to consolidation mode, where I was just doing contests and one hour of LeetCode every day until I reached around ~350 problems before my interviews. In the last month, I focused on shoring up my ML knowledge as described in the previous answer.

What is your secret in the Googleyness round?

I think the main idea is to be yourself and be authentic in your answers. In this round, I was asked behavioral and situational questions. For the latter I tried to answer it logically based on my own experience. For the behavioral component, I had prepared standard behavioural questions I found on the internet with examples from work, and also revised different projects on my resumé so I could talk about the challenges and choices I made in the project and my learnings. Discussing these answers with friends is recommended as they can point out bad answers.

How do you prepare for LeetCode? When you have a hard Leet-Code problem and you can't solve it, what do you do? Would you spend two hours working on them or do you read solutions? For each problem, do you solve them multiple times or just one time?

For LeetCode, my approach was to first explore the different boards on LeetCode premium (recursion, arrays, binary search etc.). This gives you good fundamentals on different approaches. For hard problems, I typically try not to take more than 30 minutes (as this is roughly the time given to you in the interview). If I don't get it, then I study the solution, implement it and then revise it in three or four days time to test my understanding. I tried to maintain a list of problems that needed a trick to solve, and also those where my approach was correct, but I didn't consider all the non-trivial cases, and couldn't get a passing solution. I would prioritize revising these problems, and then move on to others when I felt sufficiently confident.

How do you prioritize which LeetCode problems to practice?

My order of prep was LeetCode Explore Boards $\longrightarrow$ Google/Facebook mock interviews $\longrightarrow$ Blind 75 list $\longrightarrow$ Contests. I tried to spend very little mental energy on choosing problems, and focused more on speed and accuracy. Often, the Google/Facebook mocks and the contests would uncover a new class of problems (for instance, interval scheduling, basic calculator etc.)I would try to solve the similar problems in one session to become comfortable, and add it to a list to review later. Mocks are a highly recommended way to cover problems in a time bound setting without wasting time on choosing problems. Before each onsite interview, I revised the company specific top 100 problems from last six months to ensure I remember tricks and nuances.

3.3 How I Got My L3 Offer

Google interview experience from LeetCode discussion.

I learned a lot by reading interview experiences on LeetCode and Blind. I wanted to post my experience interviewing with Google and PayPal. My way of giving back :). This is my first post. Profile : 1.5 YoE (1 yr in PayPal), Microsoft from Top 20 in CS school.

Google SWE in ML Position. I applied online without referral. I felt extremely lucky to get a callback. Maybe it was because I applied within a few hours of the position being posted.

Interview Process
- Phone Screen 1 : 1 LeetCode style problem. Sliding window types.

  I did not get the correct intuition first. Interviewer gave me a hint. I used it well and came up with a good solution. Clean code and worked through a few examples as well.

  Should've barely scraped through I guess.

- Phone Screen 2 : 1 LeetCode style problem. Heap and sorting.

  Did very well. Got optimal solution immediately. Wrote Clean code and worked through couple of examples (noticed and fixed a minor bug while doing this, interviewer appreciated that)

- Virtual Onsite: 4 rounds plus behavioral

- Coding: 1 LeetCode style problem: started with LeetCode easy. I coded it up very quickly paying attention to naming, indentation, and dry run with example. Then he modified the problem to Leet-Code medium. Discussed two approaches (linked lists and hash maps), pros and cons. Coded linked lists approach. Was 95% done with code.

- Coding: 1 LeetCode style problem. BFS with added logic. Got super confused at first. Interviewer helped to get on track. Got the final logic in an 'aha' moment about 15 to 20 minutes into the interview. Feared not having enough time but managed to code it up quickly and quite well. Missed a couple of corner cases though. Interviewer pointed them out. I guess the interviewer must have given not bad/decent feedback at best. This was my worst round.

- Behavioral Round: Fun. Prepped all standard behavior questions. Half of the questions were completely new, half were expected. Did very well.

- ML theory : A broad general ML prompt based on recommendation (more like ML system design question). Discussion for 40 minutes on various ideas, including pros and cons. Focused on DL more than ML

- ML theory : A broad general ML prompt based on NLP

  Discussion for 40 minutes. Focused on all the latest NLP approaches (transformer, LSTM) discussed the pros and cons of each.

ML rounds went well but are subjective I guess. Coding was above average (at best). So was super anxious for result. But finally got L3, didn't clear bar for L4.

How did you prepare for interview?
- Programming: LeetCode (~137, 70% med, 20% easy, 10% hard). Read CTCI and EPI occasionally (focussed on Leet more). Though, I didn't start from scratch as I had competitive programming experience from school (CodeChef and Informatics Olympiad)

- ML: My Microsoft focused on ML, so prepped with my NLP, ML, and DL course material. Lots of great online courses available too. Stanford CS 229, CS 231n, 224n. MIT DL course

- I also read a lot of online blogs. I've given some links below (focused my prep on NLP because PayPal told me the team worked on NLP):

  - http://machinelearningmastery.com/
  - https://colah.github.io/
  - workera.ai[4]
  - mygreatlearning.com[5]
  - Glassdoor MLE interview questions

- One of my strong points in interviews is great communication. I always try to keep the interviews more conversational than Q & A types, of course, while demonstrating the technical skills. I had also prepped well, so was quite confident and optimistic in the interviews.

---

[4]https://workera.ai/resources/machine-learning-algorithms-interview/
[5]https://www.mygreatlearning.com/blog/nlp-interview-questions/

- Chose Google. A dream come true moment. I hope this experience is useful to someone. I especially felt that SWE in ML experiences were lacking, so hopefully, this post adds value there. Best of luck to everyone else prepping! Stay positive :)

3.4   How I Got Offers from Google and Facebook

An interesting story about how my friend (Mark) got his Facebook (MenloPark) E5 MLE offer.

Background

Mark is a teachlead in a start-up with 3 to 4 years of experience. He has a pretty bad work life balance and is undercompensated. There is also limited growth for him in his current company and industry.

Motivation

I really wanted to find a new job, so I pushed myself to do whatever I think is needed.

Taking Notes for Everything

I took a lot of notes and tried to summarize question patterns before each interview if I had time. For LeetCode, I had a spreadsheet[6] like you suggest. In the spreadsheet, I noted the tricks that help solving problems. For design questions, I drew small diagrams with key components and short notes. I also wrote down stories for behavior questions. Before the interview, I reviewed and skimmed through these diagrams and notes.

Practice

In total, I spent one year preparing. This was my first time interviewing with big tech companies. I was not familiar with the process. It was also my habit to be thorough. I wanted to know what the interviews would be like and prepare accordingly. The more I prepared, the more I realized there were a lot of things I didn't know. Then I met you and my preparation changed significantly. I studied with a group of friends. We practiced a lot. Six weeks before the onsite, I focused on interviews

---

[6]https://mlengineer.io/common-leetcode-questions-by-categories-532b30113
0b

intensively and deprioritized other engagements. I studied with a group of friends, to whom I would like to send huge thanks.

Onsite Strategy

When scheduling onsite interviews, I had Google, Facebook, Tiktok, LinkedIn, Roku and another one. I scheduled all of them in 2 weeks so I can negotiate offers with multiple companies at the same time. I knew Google is slower so I had their onsite early. I also interviewed with those that I had less preference first to practice and improve. I tried to be better after each interview and immediately incorporated feedback from previous interviews into the following ones. I learned a lot during these two weeks of interviewing with big-tech companies through talking with their experienced interviewers.

How much time did you spend on preparation? How do you divide time for system design, behavior, ML design?

I didn't have a specific ratio. I started with LeetCode, behavior. Then I worked on ML design and System Design interviews in parallel.

How do you prepare for LeetCode?

I started LeetCode around 2020 November. After a couple of months, I did my first phone screen with Facebook. I did about 300 LeetCode questions. I worked on LeetCode intensively until July 2021. Afterwards, I tried to solve LeetCodes when I was freed from preparing for ML and System Design interview.

How do you prepare for ML and System Design Interviews?

When preparing for ML and System Design Interviews, I set goals, i.e, "within 2 days finish reading topic A/B" or finish four chapters this weekend. I usually ended up completing only two chapters. I focus on ML design first then system design then do mock interviews.

Did you do any mock interviews? Are they helpful?

I also did ML design mock interviews with your friends. I also mock-interviewed on `interviewing.io` for behavior, system design and ML design. I incorporated feedback and tried to read books/online-courses to fill the gaps that interviewers pointed out to me. I alternated mock interviews between system design and ML design, so that I could improve them in parallel.

What other resources do you find helpful?

For system design, I used *Grokking System Design*, Alex Xu's *System Design Book*[7] and mock interviews on `interview.io`. For ML, I read papers, git repository, blogs on NLP and computer vision. I was most concerned was about depth. I tried to go as deep as possible.

How much did your current day-to-day work help with your prep?

My machine learning experience helps a little bit but NOT much. I used BERT but in the interview, we mostly just mentioned BERT but not critical and not in detail. My system design experience doesn't help much.

---

[7]`https://amzn.to/3nhSAsM`

4   LinkedIn

4.1   LinkedIn MLE Interview 2021 Part 1: Overview

In this interview series, I summarize my discussion with my friends and acquaintances about their interview experiences.

The onsite interview has five rounds. We will focus on LinkedIn specific rounds: Data Mining, Product Design and Data Coding.

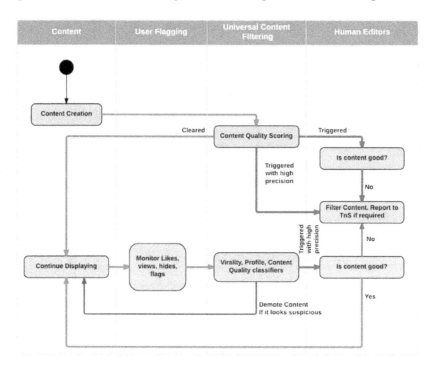

Data Mining

This round has two parts: the first part is about you and your past projects. You will want to demonstrate the impact of your project, how you come up with your solution, data, features and modeling technique. The second part will be a discussion about how you can use ML to implement some LinkedIn features. For example, you might be asked to implement job recommendations, people you may know or feed ranking[1].

---

[1]https://www.educative.io/courses/machine-learning-system-design

Data Mining Product Design

This round will dive deep into how you solve one specific LinkedIn feature using ML. It's important to address the problem from end-to-end: including which data will be useful for your model, how do you collect data for modeling, which model technique would you use and why, how do you serve and iteratively improve it.

Some examples for you to practice: design people you may know (suggest connections), hashtag suggestions when you post on LinkedIn, how to build knowledge graphs and detect technical skills.

Data Coding

This round is my favorite. Instead of asking popular questions on LeetCode, you will be asked to implement some problems that you might face in practice. Some examples you can think of are: implement variance for streaming data, implement k-means, implement logistic regression, implement some popular sampling technique, implement matrix multiplication etc.

I have working code that you can check on GitHub[2].

Summary

- Review your most proud project, understand the impact and why you come up with your solution.

- Learn about interviewer expertise by looking at their profile. Learn about basic features in LinkedIn and how you might implement them.

- Practice LeetCode questions, pay attention to questions with the tag "Random"[3]. In addition, make sure to read about my LeetCode preparation[4].

- Stay curious and try to learn about them as much as possible.

---

[2]https://github.com/khangich/machine-learning-interview/tree/master/sampl e

[3]https://leetcode.com/tag/random/

[4]https://mlengineer.io/common-leetcode-questions-by-categories-532b30113 0b

4.2   LinkedIn MLE Interview 2020/2021 Part 2: Data Coding

In this interview preparation series, I outlined the most common questions I learned from my friends who interviewed at LinkedIn for a Machine Learning Engineer position.

Data Coding Common Questions
- Random Pick with Weight[5] (uses CDF): you need to be mindful if the sum of weight is less than 1. This is a very practical question for MLE. I actually see this problem on my technical stack. Unfortunately, this question is also overused among many companies. In the future, I would not be surprised if companies stop asking this question. In case you're curious about the application of this question you can click on the below diagram.

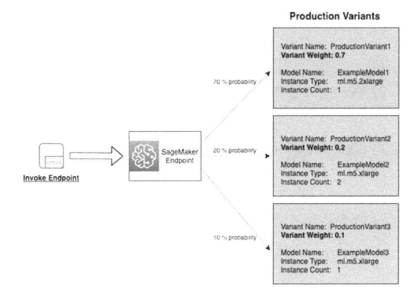

SageMaker A/B testing

---

[5] https://leetcode.com/problems/random-pick-with-weight

- Implement `rand10()` using `rand7()`[6] (uses Rejection Sampling): Given the API `rand7()` that generates a uniform random integer in the range [1, 7], write a function `rand10()` that generates a uniform random integer in the range [1, 10]. You can only call the API `rand7()`, and you shouldn't call any other API. Please do not use a language's built-in random API. If you understand this table below you can solve this problem.

	1	2	3	4	5	6	7
1	1	2	3	4	5	6	7
2	8	9	10	1	2	3	4
3	5	6	7	8	9	10	1
4	2	3	4	5	6	7	8
5	9	10	1	2	3	4	5
6	6	7	8	9	10	*	*
7	*	*	*	*	*	*	*

- Other questions: Random Pick with Blacklist[7], Random Pick Index[8] (Reservoir sampling) and Find Median from Data Stream[9] (you can replace Medium by average, variance etc).

4.3   LinkedIn MLE Interview 2020/2021 Part 3: Product Design

In this interview preparation series, I outlined the most common questions I learned from my friends who interviewed at LinkedIn for a Machine Learning Engineer position.

The Product Design round is more difficult than other rounds. LinkedIn AI has multiple ML teams work on LinkedIn features.

---

[6]https://leetcode.com/problems/implement-rand10-using-rand7
[7]https://leetcode.com/problems/random-pick-with-blacklist/
[8]https://leetcode.com/problems/random-pick-index/
[9]https://leetcode.com/problems/find-median-from-data-stream/

System Architecture

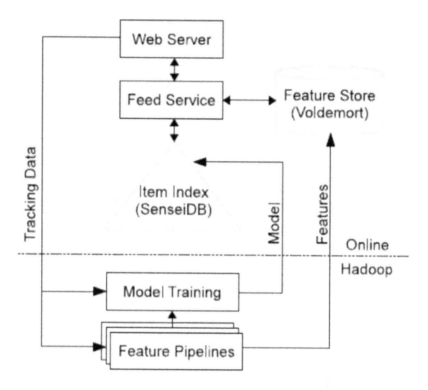

Figure 7: System architecture (simplified).

Feed AI

You will be asked to design LinkedIn features using ML related to LinkedIn home feeds: ranking and personalization. You should be familiar with techniques like Learning to Ranking, Explore/Exploit, Deep Learning, and Reinforcement Learning, coupled with multi-objective optimization and supply-demand analysis.

You can prepare for this round by reading through the following documents.

- LinkedIn Feed Ranking[10]

- Constrained Optimization for Homepage Relevance

- Understanding dwell time to improve LinkedIn Feed Ranking[11]

- People You May Know (PYMK)

- LinkedIn FeedRanking[12] on the `educative` ML System Design course

Ads AI

You will design features related to member personalization for all ad formats, placements, and objectives; marketplace optimization via targeting, bidding & budget pacing, and pricing algorithms. You might want to know some techniques in deep-learning, active learning, bandits, auction design, multi-objective optimization, graph algorithms, as well as building low-latency systems to serve these complex models in real time.

- Budget pacing for online ads

- Distributed training deep learning model

Jobs Marketplace AI

Use cases around designing an auction mechanism that determines the set of jobs to be shown on all paid job inventory on LinkedIn, and blending the paid and organic jobs to deliver value commensurate with spending, while ensuring high engagement from tens of millions of job seekers.

- Recruiter recommendation[13]

---

[10]https://www.slideshare.net/bodlaranjithkumar/activity-ranking-in-linkedin-feed

[11]https://engineering.linkedin.com/blog/2020/understanding-feed-dwell-time

[12]https://www.educative.io/courses/machine-learning-system-design/g7DrxM64mxZ

[13]https://engineering.linkedin.com/blog/2019/04/ai-behind-linkedin-recruiter-search-and-recommendation-systems

- AI behind LinkedIn jobs[14]

Fraud & Anti Abuse
Comment use cases include identifying patterns in large scale attacks and taking them down proactively before attackers get a chance to engage in nefarious activity.

- ML behind fighting harassment at LinkedIn

- Automated Fake Account Detection at LinkedIn

- Fighting abuse at scale[15]

Standardization
LinkedIn AI relies on a lot of standardized data from multiple sources. At the heart of this is the LinkedIn knowledge graph.

- LinkedIn knowledge Graph[16]

- ML in LinkedIn knowledge Graph[17]

Segments AI
These team partners help LinkedIn grow internally. Common use cases include Feed Ranking, Notifications, People You May Know, Follow Recommendations, and Job Recommendations.

- Building communities around interests on LinkedIn[18]

Communities AI
Design features in LinkedIn Video Stories, Content Discovery, and Content Quality.

---

[14]https://engineering.linkedin.com/blog/2019/02/learning-hiring-preferenc
es--the-ai-behind-linkedin-jobs

[15]https://atscaleconference.com/videos/fighting-abuse-scale-jenelle-bra
y-and-carlos-faham/

[16]https://engineering.linkedin.com/blog/2016/10/building-the-linkedin-kno
wledge-graph

[17]https://www.linkedin.com/pulse/machine-learning-linkedin-knowledge-gra
ph-qi-he/

[18]https://engineering.linkedin.com/blog/2019/06/building-communities-aro
und-interests

5 Other Interview Experience and Tips

5.1 MLE Interview at StitchFix

How to get an offer from one of the best online recommendation company in the world.

Application

A hiring manager contacted me via LinkedIn. The first call with the hiring manager is a typical screen call. We talked about my projects and my contributions etc. She was smart and asked the right questions. I was pretty impressed. I think the main reason is my LinkedIn profile has keyword "recommendation".

Phone Interview

This phone call is about 45 minutes discussion about designing a machine learning use case. I formulated it as binary classification and was able to talk end-to-end from training to serving and testing. I went on to the onsite round.

Onsite Interview

- Virtual Onsite Interview—Five rounds duration, each interview round lasted between 45 minutes to 1 hour.

- Round 1—This round tested the ML design for one specific use case. The use case is about the new online business of Stitchfix based on recommendations for customers. This is not an easy problem. I thought I was doing ok. One of the interviewers seemed to agree with the solutions. This is quite similar to the ML system design rounds at other companies. If I can do this again I would review multi-arm bandit and A/B testing more thoroughly.

- Round 2—During this round I met with the Marketing Manager. This round focused on behavior. They wanted to explore how candidates collaborate with people from different backgrounds etc. I approached this round by telling specific stories from my past experience in the STAR format. One way to prepare for this round is to practice your past stories about how you collaborated with people with different technical backgrounds. You can learn more about STAR method here.

- Round 3—This was a coding round focused at data serialization and data deserialization. This round is not LeetCode and was pretty straightforward. If you have SWE background, it's easy.

- Round 4—This is the scikitlearn/pandas round. I was given a dataset and asked to work on this dataset by showing some data analysis and train a simple regression model. I used Jupyter notebook on my laptop and I shared my screen. This round is pretty straightforward if you work with Pandas/Scikitlearn regularly. The key is to pay attention to details: outlier values, empty values and how to interpret the model metrics etc.

- Round 5—This round is quite similar to the behavior round but we also discussed ML breadth. I met with a DS manager and we discussed ML and behavior. I don't remember too much of the details for this round.

Preparation
- Machine learning—I have about four years of experience with hands-on Machine learning in practical projects. I was familiar with pandas/scikitlearn and the tensorflow stack. You can see my list of ML topics here.

- Behavioral—I didn't prepare anything specifically but I followed the Amazon STAR format and tried to tell specific stories during behavior rounds.

Key to Success
At that time I already got one offer from a small start-up after a string of rejections from FAANG[1]. I didn't know much about Stitchfix and I felt really relaxed about the whole process. I think it played a significant role in getting an offer.

I have built recommendation models from end-to-end for a few years. I also contributed to open source projects in AI/DS industry recently.

---
[1] https://mlengineer.io/from-google-rejection-to-40-offers-71337a224ebe

I think my background is generally a good fit with what Stitchfix was seeking.

Offer

I got an offer after a couple of days. Stitchfix pays their data scientists/MLEs really well. They tried to stay competitive in getting talent by giving total compensation that is close to top companies (FAANG).

At the time, Stitchfix didn't allow working remotely so I decided to pass the offer and continue with my job search.

Summary

- Stitchfix pays very well and didn't ask a lot of LeetCode questions. If you have good ML experience and ML fundamentals you can apply without grinding through 200 LeetCode questions.

- Stitchfix data science blog is one of the best in the industry. They write a lot of cool stuff. I don't know what it's like to work internally but most people I met there are smart and genuinely friendly.

- Some interesting posts from Stitchfix blogs: Nearest Neighbor Descent[2], Large Scale Experiment[3], Multi-Armed Bandits[4], What Color is it?[5]

5.2 Coupang Machine Learning Interview Experience, 2021

How to get an offer from one of the biggest e-commerce companies in the world.

Application

Recruiter contacted me via LinkedIn. After a couple of weeks, I had my phone screen for a Senior SWE, ML position.

---

[2]https://multithreaded.stitchfix.com/blog/2020/05/22/algo-hour-nearest-neighbor-descent/
[3]https://multithreaded.stitchfix.com/blog/2020/07/07/large-scale-experimentation/
[4]https://multithreaded.stitchfix.com/blog/2020/08/05/bandits/
[5]https://multithreaded.stitchfix.com/blog/2020/10/13/what-color-is-this-part-2/

Phone Interview

This phone interview has two LeetCode questions. Both questions are directly from LeetCode. The second question involves dynamic programming (DP) with 3 dimensions. I had to rush through the solution and went over time by about five minutes. I think this one is easily the hardest phone interview I ever had.

Onsite Interview

- Virtual Onsite Interview—four rounds duration. The interview consisted of three technical rounds of between 45 minutes to 1 hour each. There is one behavior round.

- Round 1—This round is purely LeetCode. It's the hard LeetCode question that requires stack as well as recursion. If you want to prepare you can practice the Basic Calculator questions.

- Round 2—This round is also LeetCode question. It's a medium 2 dimensions DP question. It's similar to string matching or substring matching on LeetCode. The second question is easier with topological sorting in graphs.

- Round 3—For the Machine Learning and System Design round, I worked on one specific ML use case end-to-end including capacity estimation. I made a minor mistake in estimating and the interviewer wasn't very happy about it. It's similar to the ranking problem in the search domain. You can find some examples in the Machine Learning System Design course.

- Round 4—I didn't do very well on the behavior round. The manager read my resumé and wanted to know my professional journey for the last ten years. If you want to prepare for it you can review your resumé thoroughly and format your answer in STAR format (see other Amazon interview stories).

Preparation

I shared my preparation at `mlengineerio.io`[6].

---

[6]https://mlengineer.io/machine-learning-engineer-interview-at-stitchfix
-8fd2f9a0c2c8

Key to Success

There were a few moments during the coding rounds where I wasn't very confident with my implementation. For example, for the 3 dimensions DP question, I know I had the right direction but I wasn't sure if I could complete it in time. I had to remind myself that I don't really need this offer; I considered this as a problem solving session and I wanted to solve this problem. I didn't care about the offer. I learned to trust my brain in that difficult moment. If you practiced well, you should trust your brain when solving a new problem. It will work out.

Offer

I got an offer after a couple of days. Coupang paid really well and they hired a lot of Google Senior SWE. Since I already got Snap's offer, Coupang was hesitant in sharing a TC number. They didn't want candidates to use their number as leverage.

5.3   How I Practiced Interviews for Pinterest MLE (2021)

Background

I'm an ML engineer with ~3 YOE, and I currently work for an e-commerce company.

In the past, I had interviewed with Snap and overall I did well on ML rounds, but not so good on the coding rounds. I felt I was underprepared for the coding part. I took a break of around 2 months then resumed my prep again in April.

The overall goal was to spend about 15 hours each week studying, while also applying and reaching out to people on LinkedIn. I ended up doing a lot of coding and ML mock interviews, in addition to interviewing with actual companies.

Coding Interview Prep

In the past, I always focused on practicing many questions and just revised the problems before the interview.

The key this time while LeetCoding was solving new problems and maintaining a note of the thought process of some very difficult problems. The goal was to be able to improve the thought process and be able to apply them even if a user problem is encountered in the interview.

I had no problems getting calls from companies, and interviewed with some companies as a warmup before the main ones where I was truly interested.

Did many mock coding rounds on the http://interviewing.io/ website mostly with interviewers from Google. I felt their questions were unseen and good level of difficulty. It made me feel confident tackling unseen problems in the interview instead of getting bogged down. Some mocks I thought I did well but got a lean no hire since your performance is always compared with other candidates' performance on the same question. For harder questions, even getting to a simple working solution was enough to get a lean hire. This experience was eye-opening. If you have a few hundred dollars to spend, I would highly recommend it.

- Sample coding question 1: You are given an array of strings, products and a string searchWord. We want to design a system that suggests at most three product names from products after each character of searchWord is typed. I suggested products should have common prefix with the searchWord. If there are more than three products with a common prefix return the three lexicographically minimum products. Return list of lists of the suggested products after each character of searchWord is typed. (A solution is linked below [7]).

- Sample coding question 2: Given an $n \times n$ binary matrix grid, return the length of the shortest clear path in the matrix. If there is no clear path, return -1. A clear path in a binary matrix is a path from the top-left cell (i.e., $(0, 0)$) to the bottom-right cell (i.e., $(n - 1, n - 1)$) such that all the visited cells of the path are 0.

  All the adjacent cells of the path are 8-directionally connected (i.e., they are different and they share an edge or a corner). The length of a clear path is the number of visited cells of this path. (A solution is linked below[8]).

ML Design
- I didn't spend a lot of effort preparing for ML interviews.

---

[7] https://leetcode.com/problems/search-suggestions-system/solution/
[8] https://leetcode.com/problems/shortest-path-in-binary-matrix/solution/

- I did around four ML mock interviews and the main takeaway was to structure the interview.

- My current work is an interesting day today. I read papers and brought new techniques to our system. I have a good sense of the Latest ML and what is going on. ML design requires a very structured way to prepare, i.e, ranking, multi-classification, trust, and safety, detect not safe content, etc. If you have a good template then you can tackle anything.

- ML fundamental rounds: I did minimal prep. Mostly covered the intro to machine learning course that one covers in university

System Design

I always felt comfortable with the system design aspect of interviews. I was very familiar with the concepts around distributed systems, fault tolerance, consistency, caching, etc. from my cloud computing course taken in grad school.

Also, I had interviewed with Snap earlier this year and did pretty well on the design round.

System design: You have certain patterns. What is the right structure and what is relevant in the problems? Certain patterns for the batch, certain from the online system. Prepare for four or five such case studies that can cover a wide range of problems.

PINS Interview Experience

- I had two coding rounds and two ML rounds.

- Coding rounds were similar to Google where questions were related to graphs, backtracking, etc

- Then there were two ML practitioner rounds. The expectation was not to come up with a full-fledged design, but I ended up talking about the requirements, metrics, ML problem formulation, ML modeling, online and offline evaluation, model serving, etc.

- The key was justifying the trade-offs at each step and explaining your choices.

- Was confident the interviews had gone well. ML rounds in particular went extremely well and I was expecting an offer. Got to know the next day, that PINS would be extending an offer.

Citadel Interview Experience

Citadel questions were harder in general (compared to both PINS and Snap). They were challenging to solve within one hour. Some questions had an element of math in them.

Citadel also asked some probability questions during the team matching phase. I don't think the candidate was expected to answer them fully since this was not for Quant SWE or Quant Research roles.

Had not explicitly prepared for math and probability questions. Answered them based on my basic understanding of probability concepts. I think I did not do too well here, but that did not affect the offer in any way, since this happened in the team matching phase and a verbal offer was already extended.

What calms you down during the interviews? I tend to perform better under pressure. That brings out the best in me.

5.4   Instacart Machine Learning Interview: What to Expect

Coding Round Interview

- These interviews are typically more difficult than a technical phone interview. The session will be platform agnostic and hosted via CodeSignal.

- Instacart has 1 or 2 coding interviews that they would like you to complete. Each session is hosted by a different engineer from our team.

- The typical coding interviews run about a one hour long. The first 5 minutes will be focused on intros and ensuring your laptop is set up. You'll have 45 minutes to complete the coding exercise. The last 10 minutes will be for Q&A

- What is sought: debugging skills, communication and presentation, overall language proficiency, modular design, code readability, testable code, ability to follow specs

- How to prepare: LeetCode.

Technical/Design

- What to expect: these are interactive conversations where the interviewer will give you a scenario at Instacart that is related to ML. The goal is to come up with an end-to-end approach to implement the functionality. You are also expected to explain the rationale behind your design, for example, the choices of models and metrics. You are welcome to use Google Draws, whiteboard, CodeSignal diagram tool (link provided by interviewer.) Feel free to choose whichever whiteboarding tool you feel most comfortable with

- What is sought: communication of ideas, asking clarifying questions, clarifying and making necessary assumptions, etc. Discuss topics like model management and monitoring, performance, business needs, scale, datastore, etc. Ability to look at trade-offs and articulate various definitions and approaches

Project Retrospective

- What to expect: this will be a deep dive into one project from your technical career and your role at the organizations that you've worked at. You may also be asked to talk about general experience, and what your interests are, and, looking ahead, where you want to direct your career.

- We'll want to dig into areas like a project you're proud of, challenges, and technical details from the project, the full process of shipping the product through to production, and the impact of the project on the user, team, or business.

- We want to understand your role on the project, and your ownership of tasks (and reports if relevant).

- Your motivation, self-awareness, empathy for others, and ability to collaborate.

- Your ability to thrive in a fast-paced, high-growth, minimal process environment

- How to Prepare: select a recent project where you had the most impact, and start at a high level about business need, stakeholders, the structure of the team, and your role within the project.

- Take the time to be introspective about your career and recall key events that have helped shape your career and have gotten you to where you are now.

- Reflect on why you are interested in joining Instacart. What makes this opportunity appealing? How does it align with your other goals?

Summary
- Code: focus on code quality (naming, readable, debug, unit-tests, etc), less dynamic program, obscure data structure.

- Design: end-to-end, trade-off, ask clarifying questions, communication skills.

- Project Retrospective: most proud project, explain your contribution and key technical decisions, demonstrate your collaboration examples, and how you manage stakeholder expectations.

5.5   One Lesson I Learned After Solving 500 LeetCode Questions

I shared my friend's (Paul) story about how to move from the hardware industry to join a FAANG-like company as a SWE.

Background
I have a Master's and about 3 years of experience using deep learning (computer vision) for a hardware company. Around the beginning of 2020, I started preparing for an interview and finally had offers from a large tech company in the Bay Area after more a year of preparation. In total I solved more than 500 LeetCode questions.

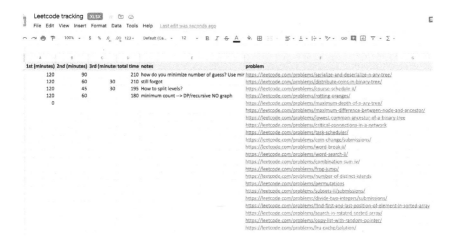

Which strategy is most helpful for your preparation?

At the beginning, I was rushing to write code, run LeetCode debugger, and read up on solutions. After that I had my interview coaching and he helped me out. When I practice I write out my thought process.

How do you prepare for system design?

I was not very successful in system design. I read the *Grokking System Design* on educative, Alex Xu's *System Design Book*[9] and *Designing Data Intensive Applications*[10] book.

How do you prepare for Machine Learning?

Some companies just ask theory questions. The Facebook ML round was different. They asked ML design (for example, Facebook recommendation) and it requires a lot of preparation. The reason I failed is because I don't have ML deployment experience. They asked some questions about embedding.

Facebook computer vision round is difficult. I was asked questions that I'm not well prepared for. I did some mock interviews with Interview Query but it didn't help much. For example, Interview Query asked questions like detect spam with Facebook photos; object detection but Facebook asked about embedding vectors.

---

[9]https://amzn.to/3nhSAsM
[10]https://amzn.to/3pooeYa

Do you need to know YOLO, mobile-net?

No you don't need to. I mentioned U-net and you don't need to have Phd, Master would be enough.

How do you prepare for coding questions?

At the beginning I just wrote the code and used a debugger. After work, with my interview coach, I wrote code on text editor (sublime), spent more time on the algorithm, and explained the logic of the algorithm. Then I spent time doing a lot of problems on the same topics before moving on to other topics.

How were your interview experience?

Uber coding evaluation: I barely passed. They rejected me after the next round; I failed because lack of ML experience.

Instacart: phone interview is LeetCode easy but my onsite system design was not good enough. For onsite, the coding question was harder (not LeetCode, but similar), the interviewer didn't give any hints. I jumped too soon to the solution. Their feedback was that I didn't solve all the coding problems, and for the system design, the interviewer thought I didn't have enough experience. I got stuck when he asked how I would design something about customer orders.

LinkedIn: for the phone screen, I don't think I did well enough. I solved the LeetCode problem, but didn't get the most optimal solution. They then asked a lot of statistics, probability and ML questions, and I couldn't answer some of the statistics and probability questions.

Adobe: I failed their onsite. There were four rounds:

1. Design Interview with a focus on optimizing at the hardware level (CPU, GPU)

2. Programming questions with a focus on analytical and problem solving skills

3. ML optimization interview with a focus on comfort level with numerics and optimization approaches (Programming or Design)

4. ML Optimization including a discussion with a focus on optimizing in the cloud environment (ML optimization, TensorRT).

I got to NVIDIA onsite multiple times with different teams, but I still got rejected.

I've done probably over 500 LeetCode problems and I still couldn't solve the problems given by Twitter (not LeetCode) and Spotify. I also applied to other companies: Google, Roblox and Snap.

If you had to start over, what is the one thing you would change?

Get coaching for coding sooner. Better to have coaches so you can benefit from the knowledge of multiple perspectives.

5.6   Airbnb Senior Data Scientist Onsite Interview

Learn how to prepare for Airbnb data science/machine learning onsite interview.

Presentation

- One About me slide: quick intro to who you are and what makes you interested in exploring this opportunity with Airbnb

- Describe a project that you worked on and/or led in the past. Ideally, select a project that had a significant business impact and that demonstrates your technical ability. We recommend about 3 to 5 slides on the problem you were trying to solve, its scope, methodology used, as well as outcomes and insights.

- Walkthrough the work you completed for the take-home challenge. You are welcome to put together slides or walk through your iPython notebook or R markdown file to present this. The team may ask questions about your code, so make sure to have this included in the presentation or easily accessible.

- Time is buffered in to allow for Q&A during and after the presentation

Coding an Algorithm Interview (60 minutes)

This interview evaluates basic fluency in Python or R programming and a general understanding of ML implementation. You'll be programming on a computer for this interview and writing some pseudo-code (more theoretical) on a whiteboard.

Practical ML (45 minutes)

You'll discuss an ML problem motivated by a particular product need in Airnbnb's Marketplace. You will be expected to propose options, analyze their strength and weakness, and refine the solution during the interview. We will be covering choices like what data you would use, how you might use it, and how you would evaluate the model's performance. We'll be assessing the stability of your approach to the task at hand, the depth of your knowledge of that approach

Algorithm/Coding

In this interview, you'll discuss an ML problem motivated by a particular product need in Airbnb's Marketplace. You will be expected to propose options, analyze their strength and weakness and refine the solution during the interview. We will be covering choices like what data you would use, how you might use it, and how you would evaluate the model's performance. We'll be assessing the suitability of your approach to the task at hand, the depth of your knowledge of that approach, and how well you understand how all the pieces of a solution fit together. To prepare, I'd suggest making sure you're familiar with Airbnb's marketplace, from the perspective of both a guest and a host.

Cross-functional Rounds

There are interviews that every candidate completes during their onsite interview at Airbnb.

Summary

- For phone interview: Visit TopCoder and if you launch the "Arena" widget, you can enter the practice rooms where you can play with the problems in the first/second division as a warm up. Airbnb Coding Challenges[11] [12]. Recommend Interview Preparation: Hacking the Interview[13], Core Java Interview Questions[14].

---

[11]https://www.hackerrank.com/test/52d6d0953bddb/357c91cd6d50039a74f53a47501e23d7

[12]https://www.hackerrank.com/test/9e26m70rtfm/cfa8b776a12fb5661055772b4297e8ca

[13]http://courses.csail.mit.edu/iap/interview/materials.php

[14]http://www.developersbook.com/corejava/interview-questions/corejava-interview-questions-faqs.php

- Algorithm and Coding: Work on a specific Airbnb features using ML, explain trade-offs of your approach, show your depth.

- Coding: similar to other LeetCode rounds at other companies.

- Cross-functional: discuss with non-technical people and focus more on your soft skills.

- Practical ML: similar to ML design round at other companies.

- Presentation: your audiences will be technical ML engineers (staff level+), focus on both business impact, demonstrate your rationale behind the solution and show your depth.

5.7   Lessons I learned from LeetCode contests

I talked with my friend Trevor (Teo) who recently has offers at Google, LinkedIn and Tiktok for Senior SWE position.

When you first started with the LeetCode contest, how many questions could you solve? How long did it take you to solve all four questions?

It's hard to say since so far I only do contests whenever I start preparing for interviews, so I can put myself in a high pressure and time constraint environment. With that said I have started with the LeetCode contest since 2017. By that time I was only able to solve 2 problems in the first several contests, where I could solve the first two problems in like 45 minutes, and often got stuck for the last 45 minutes on problem 3. After that I was able to consistently solve 2.5 problems on average (which means sometimes 2 sometimes 3 problems). I never dreamt of doing 4 problems by that time.

For this round of interview preparation, I've attended around 10ish contests over the course of 3 months. Being rusty, I was able to do 2 problems only for the first 2 contests, then consistently 3 problems, and I was able to solve 4 of them in the last three contests within around 50 mins. I have the feeling that I got lucky that those last few contests are not as difficult as others, but those results for sure boost up my confidence in interviews along the way.

What is the biggest lesson you learned by doing LeetCode contests? How do you learn to become more efficient?

Lesson learned for me is still the same old one: Practice makes perfect! It's very important that you're able to cover the most common patterns. Keep in mind that there are (easy/ medium) key problems/ tricks that you can employ in problem 3 or 4 from time to time. Once you master those tricks/ techniques, you can use those as helper functions to solve more challenging problems.

Do you think doing contests is helpful for interviews?

I think in general it helps a lot, at least for me. Though I'd have to emphasize that there are different skills required between a contest and an interview. For example, an interview question might intentionally be provided in a vague form, and it requires the interviewee to communicate with the interviewer to clarify the question and determine the edge cases. During an interview, you're also expected to think out loud and share your thought process with the interviewer. Being silent might lead to points being deducted from your overall evaluation. To some interviewers, each time they have to give you a hint also means points being deducted as well. In that sense, it really depends on the interviewer. None of these would occur in a contest.

Also, it's very important that you sleep enough before the interviews, else you might be "brain dead" quickly after a couple interview rounds.

Do you think problem 4 is relevant for interviews?

I think if you can consistently solve 3 problems in a contest (which means 1 easy and 2 medium problems in 90 minutes), then it should be more than enough for interviews.

However, I also notice that more and more companies, not just FANNG, start to ask hard level LeetCode questions, even on phone interviews. Therefore, if time permitted, I'd advise you to go over as many classic hard LeetCode questions as possible. You can set a fixed time for solving them, and read the solutions right after. You'd learn a lot of tricks/ techniques, as well as improve your ability to look at problems from different perspectives that way. I am also forming a good habit, which is to spend a bit more time after each contest to go over the solutions of the top contestants while the problems are still fresh in my mind.

5.8   Machine Learning Interview at Intuit 2020/2021

In this interview series, I summarize my discussion with my friends and acquaintances about their interview experiences.

Unlike other big tech company, Intuit has very specific way to interview for ML/DS position. During the onsite , you will have one round called CraftDemo.

Craft Demo
- ML challenge: in this 90 minutes session, you will work on a practical problem in a Jupyter notebook. Intuit prepares all the necessary code and data for you to implement some popular ML technique. It can be either linear algebra (implement transpose, matrix multiplication) or building a classifier using Keras API for a specific dataset. During this session you can use Google, Stackoverflow etc.

- After this session, you will present your solution to a panel of 4, 5 interviewers. You will need to show your solutions works, trade-off and prepare to answer any follow up questions.

- Within this session you might find yourself working with Python to handle text/binary file, how to present matrix efficiently, how to optimize for memory etc.

How to Prepare for CraftDemo?
- Know how to implement ML related algorithm: matrix multiplication, matrix transpose, K-means[15], using Keras API to solve ML problem end to end.

- Understand behind the core concept in DL and how to implement feed forward network.

- Understand how to handle big data[16] (using Spark, Map Reduce etc). One good example is how to join big data with small data, how to implement PageRank in Map Reduce.

---

[15]https://github.com/khangich/machine-learning-interview/blob/master/sam ple/kmeans.ipynb
[16]https://github.com/khangich/machine-learning-interview\#big-data

Reference

Matrix with sparse format Matrix multiplication with map Reduce

Other Interview Rounds

Intuit doesn't rely on LeetCode question heavily. Typically there will be 2–3 LeetCode questions at most. As a machine learning engineer, you're expected to understand basic statistics and how to use it to solve some statistics questions. You can find more details here[17]. I will also list ML specific LeetCode question in the next posts.

There will be about 10–15 minutes where you present your past projects. I don't think this round is difficult, you can apply the STAR technique[18] to structure your presentation.

Summary

- Review how to implement certain functions: matrix multiplication[19], k-means[20] etc. Understand how to optimize memory when dealing with big data.

- Review big data process with Spark, review map reduce for example: Word count, PageRank.

Craft Demo Checklist
Reference

Matrix with sparse format Matrix multiplication with map Reduce

MLE Onsite Interview: One Week Checklist

As the onsite day gets closer, I'm usually getting more and more uncomfortable thinking "did I miss something?" I wrote a "general check list" so I can review before the onsite.

Here is the checklist that helped me get multiple offers from top companies: Google, Snap and Coupang. Disclaimer: I also have more

---

[17] https://github.com/khangich/machine-learning-interview\#statistics-and-probability
[18] https://www.amazon.jobs/en/landing_pages/in-person-interview
[19] http://www.mathcs.emory.edu/~cheung/Courses/554/Syllabus/9-parallel/matrix-mult.html
[20] https://github.com/khangich/machine-learning-interview/blob/master/sample/kmeans.ipynb

Stage	Tasks
Data exploration	Check missing data.
Data exploration	Handle missing data: fillna, dropna.
Data exploration	Check imbalance data.
Data exploration	Handle imbalance data.
Feature Engineering	Handle categorical columns.
Feature Engineering	Detect random columns.
Feature Engineering	Should we use random columns in our feature set.
Feature Engineering	Detect label leakage information.
Feature Engineering	Exclude label leakage information.
Feature Engineering	Handle text columns.
Model training	Split train/test properly.
Model training	Pick the right metrics and can explain why.
Further improvement	If you have more time, for example 1 day or 1 week, what would you do to improve.
Discussion	What product features, real world application you can build from this exercise.

Table 5.1: Summary table

in-depth different checklists for specialized areas , i.e, Recommendation System, Feed Ranking etc. I will publish in another post.

If you prefer to review concepts by watching videos, you can check out my "one week checklist" playlist at the end of this post.

System Design
- Load balancer: load-based, round robin, active-active, active-passive.

- SS-tables vs LSM-tree.

- B-tree: pros and cons.

- Column oriented storage: pros and cons.

- Thrift and Protocol Buffers: how to handle backward/forward compatibility.

- Cache: Write through vs look-aside

- Replication implementation: statement based, WAL shipping, Logical log replication

- Partitioning: key-range, hash of keys, combine keys.

ML Fundamentals

K-means

- Initialization methods: random (2 methods)

- Time complexity: $O(n * *(dk + 1))$ if k and d is fixed. Llooyd algortihm O(nkdi) where I is number of iterations needed.

- K-means++

- MapReduce implementation[21]

- How spectral k-means works?

Logistic Regression

- Multi Colinearity: what it is and how to handle.

- Optimizer: LBFGS[22].

- Implementation: Map-Reduce[23] and ADMM[24]

Metrics

- Precision, Recall, F1, accuracy

- R2 metrics[25]

---

[21] https://pvs.ifi.uni-heidelberg.de/software/mrstreamer/k-means-example

[22] https://aria42.com/blog/2014/12/understanding-lbfgs

[23] https://srijarkoroy4u.medium.com/map-reduce-and-data-parallelism-ae038 99625fe

[24] https://www.slideshare.net/derekcypang/alternating-direction

[25] https://towardsdatascience.com/wth-are-r-squared-and-adjusted-r-squar ed-7b816eef90d9

L1/L2

- L1 tends to shrink coefficients to zero whereas L2 tends to shrink coefficients evenly. L1 is therefore useful for feature selection, as we can drop any variables associated with coefficients that go to zero. L2, on the other hand, is useful when you have collinear/codependent features.

Bias vs Variance

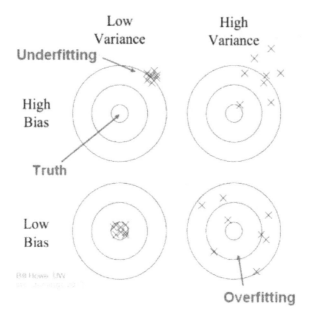

- High training error $\longrightarrow$ high bias $\longrightarrow$ Train longer, More complex model, More features, Decrease regularization.

- High cross validation error $\longrightarrow$ high variance $\longrightarrow$ More data, Decrease number of features, Increase regularization

Deep Learning (optional)

- Explain gradient vanishing and exploding. Example: Vanilla RNN, LSTM.

- What is local optimal? How many weights at each layer, why relu better than sigmoid/tanh, write down back prop formula, chain rules.

- Optimizer: Adam vs Adagrad vs RMSProp.

- Factorization machine[26]: Good to model feature interaction even in sparse data. Run fast linear $O(kn)$.

- Word2Vec[27]: Skipgram vs. CBOW.

The One Week Video Playlist

This playlist contains all the concepts and you can just watch these 23 videos and be confident about your ML fundamental interview round.

5.9   Machine Learning Design Interview

For Machine Learning engineers, ML design is the important round in final interviews. My course in ML System Design is now launched on `educative.io` and `interviewquery.com` to help candidates be better prepared and know how to approach ML design.

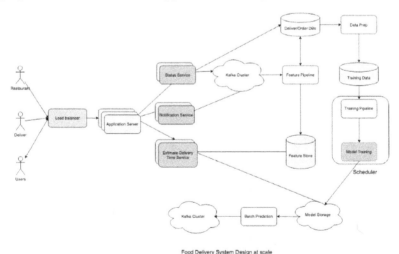

Food Delivery System Design at scale

---

[26] https://www.jefkine.com/recsys/2017/03/27/factorization-machines/\#:~: text=Introduction,with\%20extreme\%20sparsity\%20of\%20data.

[27] https://web.stanford.edu/~jurafsky/slp3/slides/vector2.pdf

What Should You Expect in a Machine Learning Interview?

Most major companies, i.e. Facebook, LinkedIn, Google, Amazon, and Snapchat, expect Machine Learning engineers to have solid engineering foundations and hands-on machine learning experience. This is why interviews for machine learning positions share similar components with interviews for traditional software engineering positions. The candidates go through a similar method of problem solving (LeetCode style), system design, knowledge of machine learning and machine learning system design.

The standard development cycle of machine learning includes data collection, problem formulation, model creation, implementation of models, and enhancement of models. It is in the company's best interest throughout the interview to gather as much information as possible about the competence of applicants in these fields. There are plenty of resources on how to train machine learning models and how to deploy models with different tools. However, there are no common guidelines for approaching machine learning system design from end to end. This was one major reason for designing this course.

The Basic 6 Steps Approach

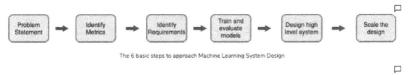

The 6 basic steps to approach Machine Learning System Design

Problem Statement

It's important to state the correct problems. It is the candidates job to understand the intention of the design and why it is being optimized. It's important to make the right assumptions and discuss them explicitly with interviewers. For example, in a LinkedIn feed design interview, the interviewer might ask broad questions:

- Design LinkedIn Feed Ranking.

  Asking questions is crucial to filling in any gaps and agreeing on goals. The candidate should begin by asking follow-up questions to clarify the problem statement. For example:

- Is the output of the feed in chronological order?

- How do we want to balance feeds versus sponsored ads, etc.?

  If we are clear on the problem statement of designing a Feed Ranking system, we can then start talking about relevant metrics like
  user agreements.

Identify Metrics

During the development phase, we need to quickly test model performance using offline metrics. You can start with the popular metrics
like logloss and AUC for binary classification, or RMSE and MAPE for
forecast.

Identify Requirements

- Training requirements

  There are many components required to train a model from end
  to end. These components include the data collection, feature
  engineering, feature selection, and loss function. For example, if
  we want to design a YouTube video recommendations model, it's
  natural that the user doesn't watch a lot of recommended videos.
  Because of this, we have a lot of negative examples. The question
  is asked:

  How do we train models to handle an imbalance class?

  Once we deploy models in production, we will have feedback in
  real time.

  How do we monitor and make sure models don't go stale?

- Inference requirements

  Once models are deployed, we want to run inference with low
  latency (<100ms) and scale our system to serve millions of users.

  How do we design inference components to provide high availability and low latency?

Train and Evaluate Model

There are usually three components: feature engineering, feature
selection, and models. We will use all the modern techniques for each
component.

For example, in Rental Search Ranking, we will discuss if we should use ListingID as embedding features. In Estimate Food Delivery Time, we will discuss how to handle the latitude and longitude features efficiently.

Design High Level System

In this stage, we need to think about the system components and how data flows through each of them. The goal of this section is to identify a minimal, viable design to demonstrate a working system. We need to explain why we decided to have these components and what their roles are.

For example, when designing Video Recommendation systems, we would need two separate components: the Video Candidate Generation Service and the Ranking Model Service.

Scale the Design

In this stage, it's crucial to understand system bottlenecks and how to address these bottlenecks. You can start by identifying:

- Which components are likely to be overloaded?

- How can we scale the overloaded components?

- Is the system good enough to serve millions of users?

- How we would handle some components becoming unavailable, etc.

6   Machine Learning Topics for Interviews

In this final chapter, I recommend the most important topics to review for your interview. You find more details about these individual projects in my second book.

ML Concept	Company	Section
Feature Embedding	Facebook, LinkedIn, Google	1.2
Sampling techniques	Facebook, LinkedIn, Google	1.3
Sampling techniques	Facebook, LinkedIn, Google	1.3
Two tower architecture, Wide and deep architecture	Facebook, LinkedIn, Google	1.5
Graph based recommendation	Pinterest	2.4
Ranknet	LinkedIn	2.2
Position Bias	Google	2.5
Calibration methods	Facebook, Pinterest	2.11
Feed Ranking	Facebook, LinkedIn	4.1
Watch Next recommendation	Youtube, Facebook	9.5

Short list of topics from the Elements of Machine Learning design book

Name	Company Offers			
Victor	Facebook			
Stanford	Facebook			
Ted	Facebook	Amazon		
Mike	Facebook	Spotify		
Jerry	Google	Facebook	Apple	Cruise
Steven	Google			
Adam	Google			
Patrick	Amazon	Wish		
Bolton	Intuit			
David	Nvidia	Nbc		
Dave	Samsung			
Daniel	Series B Start Up			
Steven	AccuWeather			
Sanchez	Pinterest	Citadel		
Ben	Amazon			
Mary	Apple	Twitter		
Mark	Facebook	Google	Tiktok	
Ariana	Intuit	Bloomberg		
Michael	Docusign			
Teo	LinkedIn	Google	Tiktok	
Neo	Facebook	Google		
Quinton	Microsoft			

Offers received by some of the people I have worked with

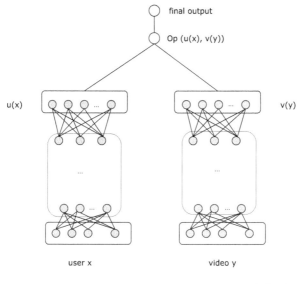

Follow my new book about Machine Learning Design at
`mlengineer.io/tagged/books` to learn about ML design for FAANG
interviews.

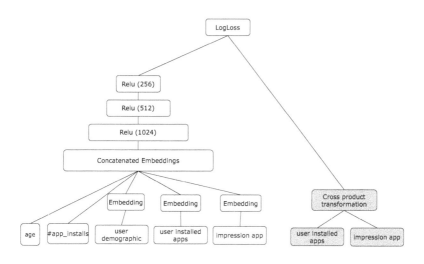